Acclaim for **John Edgar Wideman**

"Wideman is now our leading black male writer and (casting the nonsense of these divisions aside) one of our very finest writers, period." —*New Republic*

"One of this country's brightest literary lights." —*Chicago Sun-Times*

"One reads Wideman knowing that one is in the presence of an author who moves intuitively and courageously, an author who plunges below the surface, an author who might not find his way back to the surface, but in the struggle for light and air, he is discovering meaning and hope, and truth, in the midst of chaos. . . . One of the best American writers of any generation." —Caryl Phillips, *Bomb*

"A writer who belongs in our permanent library." —*The New York Times*

"The absence of personal exchanges between fathers and sons has never been so insightfully described . . . a masterpiece . . . constructed with an abundance of wisdom." —*Los Angeles Times Book Review*

"Wideman has set himself a daunting task in this book—one he accomplishes in prose that is always eloquent, often lyrical." —*San Francisco Chronicle*

Also by **John Edgar Wideman**

John Edgar Wideman

Fatheralong

John Edgar Wideman is a two-time winner
of the PEN/Faulkner Award. He lives in
Amherst, Massachusetts.

Fatheralong

A Meditation on Fathers and Sons,
Race and Society

John Edgar Wideman

Vintage Books

A Division of Random House, Inc.   New York

To my father
Edgar Lawson Wideman
and my sons
Dan
Jake

First Vintage Books Edition, September 1995

Copyright © 1994 by John Edgar Wideman

Special thanks for the research of historians Lowry Ware and the late Sidney
Kaplan, and also to Elizabeth Rauh Bethel, author of *Promiseland* (1981), and
to Winthrop D. Jordan, author of *Tumult and Silence at Second Creek* (1993).

The Library of Congress has cataloged the Pantheon edition as follows:

Wideman, John Edgar.
Fatheralong: a meditation on fathers and sons, race and
society / John Edgar Wideman
p. cm.
ISBN 0-679-40720-0
1. Wideman, John Edgar—Family. 2. Afro-American authors—20th
century—Biography. 3. Fathers and sons—United States—Biography.
4. United States—Race relations. 5. Afro-American men—Biography I. Title.
PS3573 126Z466 1994
813'.54—dc20
[B] 94-6220
Vintage ISBN: 0-679-73751-0

Manufactured in the United States of America
10 9 8 7 6

Contents

Ever splitting the light! How often do they strive to divide that which, despite everything, would always remain single and whole.

—Goethe

Common Ground

IF A CERTAIN KIND OF CAMERA, YET TO BE INVENTED, achieved the capacity to record the instantaneous give-and-take between two black people meeting in the street, looking at the artifact this "camera" produces you would see the shared sense of identity, the bloody secrets linking us and setting us apart, the names flapping in the air —black, negro, african american, colored, etc., etc. — we sometimes answer to but never internalize completely because they are inadequate to describe the sense of common ground we exchange at this moment. We acknowledge the miracle and disgrace of our history in the twinkling of an eye, many, many times a day as we meet each other, nodding or speaking or touching or just passing by, seemingly without a glance. Our ancient styles of gliding through the air can say enough, say everything that needs to be said. We are linked. I know something about you and you know something about me. Personal, intimate, revealing knowledge though we may never have set eyes on one another before nor will again. To our everlasting shame and glory what we may recognize first is something we are not. And then because of, in spite of that, something we are: survivors, carrying on.

ALWAYS MORE TO US THAN MEETS THE EYE. OUR EYES or the eyes of others who don't want to know what the more might be, who expend a lot of energy pretending there isn't more, insisting there must not be more. We carry the burden, the responsibility, the challenge and joy of creating the little extra, the something more that keeps us not exactly what we're supposed to be. What the novelist Richard Wright called a battle between blacks and whites over the nature of reality begins here, where we make up ourselves, the imagined space we preserve for ourselves and share with those others who would love us. If we're different, who decides the meaning of that difference? Who shall create its form and who shall benefit from it?

The person like me because we are both different is sharing the work of giving meaning to difference. The ones who appear like us, whom we meet in the street, are other answers-in-progress coping for better or worse with the puzzle of our identity. Although we can pretend not to, we see ourselves in them. How do we sustain within ourselves the determination, grit, the voice saying yes, we can do it, yes. Not only am I surviving, out here doing, as you see, my thing, but there's more, more to me, and I'm doing that work too. Being *me*, not what difference makes of me.

AMERICANS OF AFRICAN DESCENT SHARE A CONTINENT, a gene pool, a history. Who we are is partly determined by this triple heritage. The complexity of each of these factors—Africa's size and ecological diversity, the gene pool's constantly percolating stew of combinations and permutations, the countless individual stories constituting the grand fabric of history—such complexity within our collective past guarantees as much variety as unity among African-descended peoples. Now consider centuries of interaction as African peoples encountered the planet beyond their home place. Clearly the potential, indeed the necessity, of diversity among African-descended people exponentially increases. Increases so drastically any attempt to define common ground is suspect.

Moving the time line backward one hundred and fifty million years to the Rift Valley in East Africa and the generally accepted genesis there of all humankind, even the notion of "African descent" loses its uniqueness. Since we all started there, the question is not if, but when. By measuring and mapping the spread of DNA markers, "microsatellites" for example, scientists are identifying waves and routes of emigration through the centuries that separated various populations from the mother continent and affected their genetic characteristics. A crucial by-product of this research is further destabilizing of conventional notions of "race."

What do we know about a person, what can we assume or predict about their behavior if they assign themselves or we assign them membership in a group whose biological, temporal, spacial origins are so ancient and have been so implacably modified, so problematically conceived and perceived, that the most substantial evidence the group exists, either in their own minds or ours, resides in the dogged efforts to define it, name it, ask questions about it, make predictions about its members.

Common ground. How can we seek it, understand it without slipping into talk about race? And once race enters the discussion doesn't a net settle over our heads, capturing nothing but destroying what passes through its deadly weave? Chaos looms because race can mean everything or nothing. A denial of diversity. A claim of profound, unalterable difference between kinds of human beings. An empty word. A word bristling with the power of religious dogma and faith. A word obsolete, anachronistic, dysfunctional in vocabularies which attempt to model a rational, holistic version of humanity here at the dawn of the twenty-first century. A word hovering like a toxic cloud, obscuring discourse at all levels, as much a problem as it was a hundred years ago when W. E. B. Du Bois predicted the major challenge confronting Europe and America in the twentieth century would be the question of race.

The discovery of people unlike themselves did not

spark in Europeans a doctrine of cultural relativity: it produced the invention of race. Of all the weapons devised to conquer and subjugate the lands beyond Europe, the most effective, pervasive, and enduring, the one that served to coordinate, harmonize, and intensify the effects of all other weapons, is the concept of race. Soldiers who wielded the broadsword, musket, Gatling gun, rockets, and bombs could slaughter, free of conscience and remorse, when the enemy belonged to a race less than human. Priests could sanction and abet the slaughter, share the booty of empire while they debated in learned councils whether or not the lesser races possessed souls. How could a race closer to wild beasts than to men own the land they occupied, govern themselves, or enter the economic life of European colonies except as slaves. The paradigm of race located within its victims the causes and justification of the victim's plight. Thus the oppressed, to the degree they internalized the message of race, became active agents of their oppression.

Dissatisfaction with European societies did produce a strain of speculation toying with the idea that the "other," the savage—American Indian, Ashanti warrior, Hottentot—might be closer to nature and thus noble in some sense. The terms of this minor dissent did not alter the hierarchical paradigm of race, the Manichaean, essentialist assumption of different kinds, different orders of men. The paradigm remained intact even though a Rousseau might switch labels, invert it.

European theories of race were elaborated, as they have been since, to rationalize prerogatives of self-interest.

By postulating in other, lower orders of beings very damaging, incapacitating, innate defects, lacunae, or wholesale global inferiority, the applications of various cures—baptism, slavery, colonization, integration, search-and-destroy, education, containment in its many forms—apartheid, segregation, reservations, prisons, homelands, concentration camps, missions—were not only reasonable but humane, divinely sanctioned duties.

In this connection, the history of how subject peoples or minorities were absorbed into dominant societies, no word has as yet emerged for people of color in America who embrace the mores of the dominant group and merge into the mainstream. *Conversos* is such a word describing Jews in fifteenth-century Spain who converted to Catholicism, rather than emigrate during the enforced ethnic and religious cleansing after Isabel and Ferdinand expelled the Moors who'd ruled Spain for six hundred years. There are plenty of nasty, vernacular, funny/bitter words for minority members who attempt either openly (integration) or clandestinely (passing) to convert, but no official term exists for those who have crossed over, perhaps because such a word would acknowledge the possibility that racial categories are permeable, not permanent. An Ethiop can't be washed white. Leopards can't change their spots, can they?

Mulatto, a word we did import from Luso-Hispanic culture with its rich vocabulary of racial designations, sounds a little like *converso* and maybe it's as close as we've ever come to adopting such a word. But *mulatto*, like *mule* or *miscegenation*, a word invented just prior to the Civil

War as part of a campaign of dirty tricks to discredit the antislavery Abolitionists, suggests a compound of immutable elements. Appearing first in a pamphlet entitled "The Theory of the Blending of the Races, Applied to the American White Man and the Negro" (1863), *miscegenation* rather quickly replaced *amalgamation* as the preferred term for propagation between blacks and whites. Amalgamation implies white and black could "unite into one body or organization." The neologism *miscegenation* eradicates the potential of biological unification, explicitly preserves in its etymology the divisive paradigm of race (Latin: *miscere* = mix; *genus* = race).

THOUGH MOST OF US HAVE BEEN CONDITIONED TO confuse race with culture, they are not synonymous. Race does not equal color, either. Nor is race the systematic description, classification, and analysis of what distinguishes one human group from another. The concept of race, whose presence continues to poison our society, gradually evolved during the long European diaspora to every part of the globe. The word *race* evokes a paradigm, a systematic network or pattern of assumptions, relationships, a model of reality, of history and causation as complete, closed, and pervasive as a religion. Race is not a set of qualities inhering in some "other," it's the license to ascribe such qualities allied with the power to make them stick. Race functions like Humpty-Dumpty's disconcerting habit of stipulating definitions: to surprise, destabilize, take control. Race can mean something or nothing or whatever lies between, an essentialist concept or an existential one, depending on the moment, the serviceability of a definition, its usefulness to the stipulator. Race is the ultimate carte blanche.

It's impossible to pin down the definition of race because race is a wild card, it means whatever Humpty-Dumpty says it means. Think of a blank screen, then seat somebody at a keyboard controlling what appears on the screen. Race is whatever the operator decides to punch up. The meaning of race is open-ended, situational, functional, predictable to some extent, but a flexible repertoire of possibilities that follow from the ingenuity of the operator privileged to monopolize the controls.

On the other hand, race signifies something quite precise about power, how one group seizes and sustains an unbeatable edge over others. When the race wild card is played, beware, the fix is in. Particularly if the word appears in a setting where some competition is occurring—a bargain, a contract, a ball game, courtroom, treaty, romance. Race is a clue, a sign the outcome is being rigged. Various unsavory, unfair maneuvers can be expected. Race in its function as wild card is both a sign and an enabler of these shady transactions in a game only one player, the inventor of race, can win. He always holds the winning cards because he can choose when he plays them and names their value.

One symptom of our national confusion, our multiple personality disorder in regard to race, is how we have severed the relationship between the word *race* and *racism* or *racist*. Daily, we depend on the notion of race to rationalize differences between blacks and whites, reinforcing the fictions these categories represent, in spite of all the evidence to the contrary, including the evidence of our eyes, hearts, and sexual equipment. Consider our mania for statistics. If racial breakdowns deliver more substance to measurements we take of ourselves, the omnipresence of race as a category in our counts makes race seem to count too much. Race appears to cause crime rather than be caused by a crime. Do black newborns die at three times the rate of white babies because of some factor intrinsic to blackness or because being black means they're treated by society as only one-third as valuable as white newborns? Race serves almost everybody as a primal means of identifying self and others, further insuring distance between blacks and whites. Yet the words *racist* or *racism* are usually applied only to those who admit out loud they like the way race serves us, especially those who celebrate, praise God, even swear they'll fight to the death to keep race dividing us as it does. In nice people's mouths race is a descriptive, normative, neutral term, and they feel free to employ it freely. Racists by definition aren't nice people; they embarrass the rest of us by giving race a bad name. "Race" and "racism" are equally predatory, destructive; one just wears sheep's clothes.

The *Bakke* decision of the U.S. Supreme Court calling into question the logic of racial quotas is a classic example of how the wild card of race can be manipulated. In now-you-see-it, now-you-don't sleight-of-hand maneuvering, the Court declares race shouldn't be a factor in college admissions or hiring, and in the next breath race is all that matters.

Civil rights legislation before *Bakke* seemed to be moving to remedy long-standing inequities, an imbalance of power and privilege that had mired a portion of the population in second-class citizenship. Implicit in the remedies were costs society would have to pay to redress the wrongs of the past. In *Bakke*, at the threshold of exacting these costs, the dues that must be paid, the Court balks. It's deemed unfair for an individual to shoulder the collective debt. Individual rights outweigh the wrongs perpetrated on a group. Who then is responsible for the price of the ticket to implement the changes civil rights legislation mandated? Bakke's "race" is ignored when it indicts him, confirmed when it benefits him. If power is to be equitably distributed, somebody must give up something. Who? When? How long?

Ironically, the paradigm of race both insists on white supremacy and renders white people curiously innocent of their "race." From the middle of the nineteenth century American whites sat, or were told they sat, by other whites, at the pinnacle of power and privilege in the most privileged and powerful nation on earth. Reflected every minute of every day to every citizen by the nation's mainstream institutions, culture, language, religion, economy, white superiority was supremely secure. White people were standard issue, nearest to God, the measuring rod for comparing other kinds of people. White might be imitated but never duplicated. Race was difference, a deficiency stigmatizing others because they weren't, never could be white. Thus, for all intents and purposes, whites viewed themselves as raceless.

The recent advent of public demonstrations of white power, neo-Nazi tribalism, the adoption of the language and techniques of civil rights protests of the sixties by white supremacist hate groups are signs of radical displacement. Unquestioned centrality and preeminence of white Americans at home and abroad are no longer secure. Barbarians are at the gates, in the adjacent neighborhood, the backyard. What once could be assumed as a birthright must now be negotiated. Others are laying claim to prerogatives that heretofore belonged exclusively to those who were "free, white, and twenty-one."

In a legal system claiming to be color-blind, white immunity to race had been no disadvantage—in fact, exactly the opposite. Since whites didn't need to go public about their race, all those court rulings favoring the white majority could be construed not as racist but simple justice. These intertwined fictions were unraveled simultaneously as courts were confronted with evidence of how race had affected their decisions. The majority's interest could no longer be treated as synonymous with everybody's interest. Or could it? If race was the basis of challenges to the legal system, why not race as the basis of a response to the challenge? The contradictions, paradoxes, fault lines in the paradigm of race were already in place. The *Bakke* business was a field where the race game could be played.

Bakke discovered or remembered he belonged to a race

after all, a race that was under assault from other races and required the Court's protection. The fiction of color blindness was temporarily suspended by the Supreme Court to allow Bakke to slip through. Then the justices serenely resumed business as usual, as if never before and certainly no longer should race matter. Switching labels, turning color blindness on its head, the operator at the keyboard punches in whatever definitions of race the justices require to spin their web, and all through the shenanigans, keeps a straight face.

Bakke is the white minstrel who corks his skin, dons a stevedore's raggedy clothes, jumps on stage, and dances Jim Crow. Disguising himself as a black man, or rather acting out a grotesque parody of a black man, Bakke becomes "whiter," the black man "blacker." His performance validates the status quo. Pretending he belongs to an oppressed race frees him to preserve the power of the oppressor.

Torn away from their continent by the international trade in slaves, Africans learned the languages of Europe and entered the conversation about race. However, what they said about themselves, or attempted to prove about themselves, affected the theorizing about race minimally because the relationship signified by the paradigm of race devalued African contributions. Conversations inevitably were one-sided, circular. Sooner or later, often with stunning, bloody impact, the exchanges, such as they were, ended with the question: who's in charge here? Listen to the anguished voices of the Xhosa in nineteenth-century South Africa or the Sioux in South Dakota during the same epoch. Consult the historical record for the responses of the European invaders of their lands. Race contained the answer, was answer, question, and end of discussion. Everything and nothing, depending on the message the technician operating the scoreboard chose to broadcast.

How can we talk about ourselves without falling into the trap of race, without perpetuating the terms of a debate we can't win because the terms of the debate already contain an understanding, a presumption of winner and loser?

A continent, a gene pool, a history, then everything else that has shaped us. The paradigm of race authors one sad story, repeated far too often, that would reduce the complexity of our cultural heritage. Race preempts our right to situate our story where we choose. It casts us as minor characters in somebody else's self-elevating melodrama.

So race ain't it. Huh-uh. The common ground is elsewhere: the bonds we struggle to sever, discover, invent, sustain, celebrate. If we pay attention, we hear many stories of black people trying to work out ways of living on the earth. Taken together the voices sing out a chorus of achievement. Whether the speaker is a photographer, dancer, stonemason, fashion designer, teacher, train engineer, listen for the moment of freedom, of self-revelation in their accounts when self merges with something greater than self. Strangely, miraculously, this detachment, this blending is also the surest sign of individuation: the power to let go, to become. To take a chance and through hard work, luck, determination, fate, joy, pride, greed, hunger, whatever—push yourself past yourself to another higher level.

Our power lies in our capacity to imagine ourselves as other than what we are. Common ground is the higher ground, spiritual and material, we strive to gain.

African-American descent plays a part in all our stories, a powerful role in many. Racism appears as a factor just as often. On the other hand, race—the doctrine of immutable difference and inferiority, the eternal strategic positioning of white over black—can be given the lie by our life stories. Racism can stunt or sully or deny achievement, but many black people are on the move, beyond the power of race to pigeonhole and cage. They are supplying for themselves, for us, for the future, terms of achievement not racially determined.

We don't have to lose to win. Don't need to prove ourselves in the no-win race game. Anybody who needs permission to be free isn't prepared for freedom. Anybody who understands how race works in this country to confuse and cripple people, black and white and every color in the rainbow, is closer to realizing things don't have to work the old way.

WE ARE IN THE MIDST OF A SECOND MIDDLE PASSAGE. To understand the scale of dislocation, violence, loss of life afflicting black communities in America today, one needs a parallel as stark and comprehensive as the Middle

Passage. Separated from traditional cultures, deprived of the love, nurturing, sense of value and identity these cultures provided, enslaved Africans in the New World found it necessary to reinvent themselves, if they were to survive as whole human beings in an alien, hostile, chaotically violent and threatening environment. Those are the precise conditions, the awesome tasks confronting young African Americans again. A configuration of devastatingly traumatic forces have severed a generation from its predecessors. The poor are most immediately at risk, though economic class alone doesn't determine which young people feel rootless, deserted, adrift in a world no one has prepared them to understand. A void behind, a void ahead, they've been abandoned in a tractless wilderness where the natural instinct to survive exacts behavior that reflects the raw, brutal circumstances trapping them. We are witnessing the spectacle of cultural breakdown, the precarious struggle of a people to emerge, to negotiate a Middle Passage with something valuable of themselves intact. This storm may destroy the entire society, or there may be in the flashes of lightning the upheaval engenders—music, new forms of bonding, revival and reexamination of heroes from the past, the celebration of self, of the sensual body, the absolute rejection of a social compact that dooms them to marginality, the militant energy, the refusal to be disrespected—a glimpse of common ground where fathers and sons, mothers and daughters can sit down and talk, learn to talk and listen together again.

It's very late in the day and frustrating to repeat the obvious, not because some people may have heard the words before, but because so many haven't.

I don't need to hate white people in order to love myself. But I also don't need white people to tell me what I am or what I can strive to be or tell me if I've made it or not. I don't need to know a white person or know of white people to make a good life for myself or be happy with myself or to love other people whatever color they may be or not be.

I do hate the paradigm of race—a vision of humankind and society based on the premise that not all people are created equal and some are born with the right to exploit others—because it gives white people unfair, unassailable advantage over me. Strands me in America at the bottom of the ladder of humankind, at worse (segregation) deprived, oppressed, condemned; at best (integration) demeaned, compromised, eternally dependent. As defined within the paradigm of race, both integration and segregation are equally unacceptable, keep me running, too busy trying to get out from under a rock and a hard place to enjoy freedom if freedom could ever be achieved.

The paradigm of race is the antithesis of freedom. It locks white people in a morally and ethically indefensible position they must preserve by force. Fosters a myth of superiority they must act out; dictates to them whom they should love and hate. Since it sanctions and reinforces the idea that some people are born better than others, deserve more than others, have an innate right, even duty, to seize from others what they want, the paradigm of race is destructive to anyone not white, and ultimately also self-destructive for whites. A racist disposition towards nonwhites, because it hardens the heart and rationalizes extremes of selfishness and brutality, inevitably reappears in the way whites regard and treat other whites. The pervasive violence in our society—from domestic abuse to economic exploitation to capital punishment to punitive expeditionary wars—is rooted in the paradigm of race.

The pieces that follow on fathers, color, roots, time, language are about me, not my "race." They are an attempt, among other things, to break out, displace, replace the paradigm of race. Teach me who I might be, who you might be—without it.

Fatheralong

P r o m i s e d   L a n d

ABOUT THREE YEARS AGO MY FATHER WAS DRIVING ME
to the Greater Pittsburgh Airport. I was on my way home
to Amherst, Massachusetts, where I live, write, and teach,
and the hour or so it took us to reach the airport and
load me aboard a plane would be the only time spent
with my father during this visit to Pittsburgh. Both my
parents reside in the city, but have not lived together for
years. When I traveled to Pittsburgh, alone or with my
wife and kids, my parents' separation complicated little
choices and big ones—where we'd stay, who would be
invited to official functions, how we'd divide our time,
whom we'd treat to a special restaurant, who'd meet us at
the airport, who'd drop us off for the flight home—all
these decisions possessed an edge of awkwardness and

3

discomfort for me because they involved exclusion, segregation.

Until quite recently my mother and father, mother more than father, really, couldn't abide being thrown together in social situations. Not a yelling, screaming, violently allergic reaction, but a palpable unhappiness. When they were stuck in the same place at the same time, my father's presence could spoil my mother's enjoyment of an occasion. He always claimed he wasn't affected by her being around or not, felt her business none of his. On the other hand he'd say he knew she minded him, and, therefore, he felt strongly obliged to honor her sensitivities by excluding himself. If pressed, she also would declare it didn't matter to her if my father showed up at a big family gathering, or sat in the audience of some public event where I might be reading or lecturing or receiving an award. I think she really meant she was willing to bear discomfort so as not to create difficulties for me or impose on others by staying away and dampening the spirit of an event. She was saying it was okay for him to be around because she'd suffered through his presences and absences most of her adult life, and she could handle it one more time.

Seeing my parents in the same room, no matter how large or small the room, I was forced to consider this history. How pain had supplied them with ample justification as well as the means to ignore each other totally. I could almost hear the hum of energy, the constant exercise of will and discipline it required for each of them to pretend the other was not in sight, could not be reached by a medium-loud *yoo-hoo*. Too many bitter memories formed a wall between them and from where I sat on stage I could hear more bricks being stacked. Two people as far apart as they could manage, without exploding the confines of the building containing them. The irony of her light complexion, his deep brown skin, as if color, too, had decided to proclaim their differences. Comical almost, how hard they worked to let everybody know they weren't together, when anyone who might notice or care had gotten the message down pat long ago. I could almost laugh sometimes. Or wished I could. One person decides another doesn't exist and is determined, with the intransigence of religious conviction, to stick to his or her guns, in spite of all evidence to the contrary, including thirty-some years of marriage, children, grandchildren, and great-grandchildren shuttling between them. Edgar and Bette bumping, tripping, literally falling over each other in a doorway or a crowded hall to stay out of each other's nonexistent way

I'd observed the slapstick stuff and nearly laughed inside, but couldn't because I'd also watched, more than once, my mother's resolve, her display of strength for my benefit—*It's all right. Don't worry Doesn't matter if he's there. I'll be fine.*—disintegrate. At the last moment she can't be coaxed out the door. *Not what you think. Youall go and have a good time. I'm just not up to going out this evening. Need to be by myself tonight.* Or me standing at a podium and one quick scan of a skimpy crowd would be enough. My father ain't showing up. Huh-uh.

Over the years the situation had gotten a little better.

In a way. Last-minute defections seldom occurred. We were all growing older. Trips to Pittsburgh rarer. Certain tactics for staying out of each other's way, through trial and error, had been formalized, ritualized by my parents. Finally, I guess we all adjusted to the notion of things being a particular way that wasn't going to change. And whether anybody liked it or not, our only choice was to accommodate ourselves. Neither pain, discomfort, awkwardness, nor the weight of memory were going to vanish, so to say things were better doesn't ring exactly true. *Easier* is not the word either. Things happen, situations repeat themselves, require you to respond again and again. You perform as you must, call on parts of yourself, mind and body, you were sure couldn't be counted upon to handle certain unthinkable tasks, but they do, once, and then more than once, and the unthinkable subsides to a kind of numbed persistence, familiar after a while, not better, not easier, as you repeat what must be done.

GOING TO PITTSBURGH MEANT STAYING IN MY mother's house, at the edge of Homewood, on Tokay Street at the foot of hills, the slope of Tokay looming almost perpendicular from its intersection with Frankstown Road a block away where Frankstown commenced its own steep climb to East Hills. Meant including my father when possible, when there was no necessity and little likelihood of my parents being thrown together too intimately. In other words, I fit him in where convenient. As much as I tried to blunt the starkness of these arrangements, my father understood as well as I did, choices had been made, lines drawn. He was marginalized. No way around it. That was that. My phone calls to him, the squeezed-in lunches or breakfasts we shared, the elaborately choreographed pop-in visits to see his grandkids, maybe outdoors when Danny and Jake were shooting baskets and Jamila was on a swing in the playground across from my mother's house, or perhaps when everybody was inside the house and my mother was out shopping, these arrangements were as much a playing out of the cruel logic of the choice I'd made to exclude him as they were expressions of concern, love.

Sometimes I felt like a pompous ringmaster in a circus, popping my whip to seize the crowd's attention, pointing to the acrobats, extolling their derring-do, so nobody would pay attention to the roustabouts sweeping elephant shit from a stage where the next act would perform.

Sometimes I just felt like shit. Drank far more than necessary, needed lots of sleep. Not sorry for myself, because I was happy to be home, enjoyed the hell out of my people, wouldn't have chosen to be any other place in the world. Yet I was also lost in an emotionally demanding terrain I had no clue how to negotiate. I worried about time. Time foregrounded as I tried to get around Pittsburgh and see everyone I wanted to see. Time a pain in the ass because it was always running out and my father still waiting to hear from us. No escape. No escape because beneath the good feelings a sad place with no bounds. Part of being happy with my Pittsburgh family was an awareness of how much I missed them, would continue to miss them as our lives played out in different directions. And missing them was also a foretaste of losing them, raising my fear of the inevitable trips back, if I lived long enough, to nursing homes, sickbeds, funerals.

The unbearable thought of losing them got mixed up with thoughts of the ones already missing, my Pittsburgh ghosts, John and Freeda French; Harry Wideman; Martha Fallon; Maya, my sister's lost baby daughter; my Uncle Otis. Those absent ones who should be weightless, immaterial, tilted the earth on its axis, and the people I loved, whom I could still touch, talk to, who hug me, pass me the corn bread, smile, remember, they spill off the edges, we all float up, become insubstantial, our time on earth foreshortened, unreal, as brief and undependable as the time of the ones who are gone. The past, present, future flatten into one chance, one chance only and then everything's gone. Always gone even as you reach out to touch. Somehow this was it. How things worked, our lives brought us to places and they were sorry-assed, baggy-pantsed, tacky, skimpy places after all, and lives happened this way, slipped away from you. People got stuck. Good moments, bad moments come and go, even high dramas, with their freight-train impact for better or worse, come and change nothing because people get stuck, stymied. Whether we know or not why we've arrived at a dead end doesn't matter because time runs out before we have the slightest notion how to change our condition, how to escape the low-grade, percolating sadness deflating our lives.

Memory, the past, prove your fuckups always catch up with you. Truth is consequences. Both. Always.

Maybe I'm taking too roundabout, too ponderous a digression to convince you that riding to the airport with my father is not a simple matter. We never discuss my ambivalence about being home, coming home, or any of the other business I've been venting, but we both understand our time together, whatever else we might desire it to be, is also sadly inadequate. These few minutes, plus or minus a few more, are what we'll have this time I'm in town, all we've had for thirty years or so since I graduated from college. An hour here, an hour there. At some level our meetings remedial, catch-up, at worst payoffs, bribes, tithes paid to sustain an illusion. What can be distilled into ninety minutes to compensate for three days in my mother's house when doing what I felt I needed to do allowed me only ten minutes to phone my father, let him know I'm in town, my schedule tight as usual, that I'll try to stop by his apartment but most likely it won't happen this trip. Everybody back in Amherst says hello. They couldn't come this time. Maybe next time, the holidays, maybe, when we're all in town we'll get together. I'm on my way to another couple cities on book business. Pittsburgh just a whistle-stop. Can barely squeeze in hello to everybody. Hello. Hello.

HIS CAR'S RUNNING POORLY, DOESN'T ALWAYS START right up, but my father thinks it will make it to the airport and back. Once it gets going it's usually fine. Engine's still strong. We'll leave early, leave time for breakfast. Hit the parkway before rush hour and that should give us a chance to sit down and talk at the airport.

My father knocks.

We're on schedule, according to plan. The morning three years ago blends with others, before and since, not always my father driving, but me wondering each time I leave the city where I grew up in houses with him or houses without him but him still paying the bills for a roof over my head, food in my stomach, wondering what it meant to see so little of him each trip. How many more trips would there be? My father not getting any younger, and me, unaccountably, impossibly, fifty-two years old, a father myself, a grandfather if one of my grown kids wills it or slips. Fear the starkest form my wondering takes, the cross-wired jolts of anticipation and dread complicating this visit and every other. Growing up and having a father and leaving and returning and leaving doesn't go on forever. Fear of losing him, that visceral fear and another kind shaped by frustration and remorse. I hadn't ever handled this business of my father very well. Couldn't. Feared the day when I'd have to answer for my failure to be a different kind of son. Still my greater fear was looking in the mirror the moment after the moment I'd lose him, when "handling it" wouldn't mean a damn thing one way or another because "it" was finally out of my hands. Distance between us finally closed.

The simple truth was I'd never worked very hard, once I became an adult, to understand my father's life. He'd chosen to live alone, apart from the household of my

mother and my siblings, and I'd left it at that. I'd gone
away, too. Far enough away so I wasn't sure how much I
cared about the particulars of his life. I loved him, wished
him health and happiness, avoided other sorts of questions. I'd learned avoidance and denial from my father.
Learned not to risk asking questions whose answers, most
likely, I wouldn't want to hear. He'd chosen to live alone
and that might be cold comfort. On the other hand,
maybe alone was preferable to getting burned. What purpose would be served by questioning his motives, as-
signing blame, admitting I missed him, needed him? If
I did.

Tina Turner sang a song my daughter Jamila was crazy
about and did a pretty impressive job of singing to herself
in her sweet, pipy ten-year-old girl's voice straining after
Tina's high notes: "What's love got to do with it . . . got
to do with it. *La-di*-something *da* . . . a secondhand
emotion."

My father knocks. It had been quiet in my mother's
house. Still dark and quiet outside when I had crept down
the steps, ducking automatically at the point I must or
bump my head into the bulging ceiling of the stairwell,
hoping I don't awaken my niece or her daughter asleep
on a bunk bed in a tiny room next to mine. I'd thought of
tier upon tier, mothers and daughters, generations asleep,
rising, no men in sight. I know my mother will be down-
stairs already in the kitchen. Coffee heating. A pot and
skillet already on the stove. Sausage, eggs, bread for toast
laid out, even though I'll say no to a hot, old-time, home-
cooked breakfast. In a banana-and-yogurt phase. She

hasn't forgotten I've changed my eating habits, my diet. Illness has modified hers too. She's my mother, she knows, but as long as she's able, she'll give me a choice, offer the old way things used to be, if I choose. She's my mother and that doesn't change. You sure now? No trouble. Everything's out and ready. Thanks, Mom. Coffee's all I ever want first thing. A banana, yogurt, or maybe some shredded wheat, later.

Yogurt in the fridge. Bananas you see on the table.

The kitchen's bright, on the counter beside the toaster oven the little black radio set to a twenty-four-hour news station babbles softly to itself like those raggedy people who wander up and down Homewood Avenue.

I'm half listening to my mother, her voice accompanied by the radio's low-decibel squawk. Time the weight of a giant thumb already beginning to snub us out. The little time we have left. She's telling tales about my nieces and nephews, my aunts, the church folks I've known since I was a baby who were her best girl friends and sick and dying now. I'm jealous, astounded as always at her skill in weaving these stories, making them real through just the right choice of detail, how precipitously and seamlessly she switches from some gossipy joke about somebody to a funeral or an unexpected teenage pregnancy then back to this or that cute thing one of her great-grandkids said, mimicked exactly, telling nonstop but never in a hurry facts about a disease. Cancer or sugar or arthritis, then describing minutely the aluminum-foil homemade false teeth a lady started wearing to church two Sundays ago: Me trying my best not to laugh at those tin teeth and my terrible sister Geraldine, you know how terrible she can be, keeps poking me and grinning over at the poor woman who doesn't know any better and keeps grinning back, showing off those godawful aluminum-foil teeth. Geraldine won't stop, and the woman flashing that tin smile every time Geral grins at her and I'm about to fall out of my seat and roll in the aisle . . .

Like kids playing tag somebody's always *it* in my mother's stories, somebody's a little crazy or desperate or too good to be true or stuck in the middle, but the game goes on, the story continues till somebody else gets tagged or tags themselves. Show don't stop for one monkey, the show goes on and I surrender, submit to the rhythm of the story's endless unraveling, not catching everything my mother says, not missing much either. Find myself caring about everything her voice touches because she clearly cares. Certain tidbits I've heard before, batted back and forth between my mother and her sisters, Martha and Geraldine, but twice-told, thrice-told is better, leaner, closer to the bone, to the voice inside my head amening, offering testimony and witness. Listening intently is also slipping away, falling half-asleep again in the kitchen, drinking coffee, helping my mother tell her stories, hearing her so deeply I'm not positive who's talking, who's listening, and don't care.

Then my father knocks and I know I must be the one to answer the door and know I shouldn't ask him in.

He says Hi. Good morning. I remember how he purses
his lips to start a smile. For an instant it seems he might
have trouble as he works his mouth to get it right. The
smile's in his eyes first, then spreads down his face. His
lips relax. Easy, after all.

I say good morning. Say I'm packed and ready to go
. . . be with you in a sec. Not opening the storm door,
blocking the doorway instead of moving aside so he
might enter. Maybe we stand this way, in the near darkness of dawn one beat or two thousand beats too long,
or maybe I just imagine he feels his entire life pass before
his eyes as I feel mine is passing, face to face in the few
moments, father and son, we need to exchange greetings.
Who is this stranger at my mother's door? At this intimate morning hour. Who is he? Who am I? The whole
endless tale passes, endless because it's all questions, delivers no answers, rushes through me like a whirlwind,
and when it's gone, not over, just gone, I truly have no
idea how long I've been standing in the hallway holding
the front door open, speaking through the screened
upper half of the storm door, waiting for my father to
turn towards the street, take the step backward he must
take so I don't have to shut the door in his face.

You have bags, don't you?

Just this little stuff here in the hall. I'll grab it on my
way out.

Your mother up?

Oh yeah. You know how she is. I'm just gonna say
good-bye and be right out.

I watch him cross the porch. Long-legged. Wearing a

blousey tan jacket. From the back I can't see his belly so he looks about the same as he did thirty or forty years ago. Solid, strong. Six foot, two hundred pounds. An athlete's bob, weave, and balance in the roll of his thick shoulders, the confident stride with the barest hit of diddy-bop, street-corner swagger, down the steps and sidewalk to his car. Don't you dare underestimate, don't you even think about feeling sorry for this man. Don't you ever assume a quarter-inch of liberty in your dealings with him that he doesn't authorize. His body speaks these words. Unambiguously as his knock, a few moments before, breaking the spell of my mother's house.

She's behind me in the hallway when I close the front door and turn around. There are times when I'm aware of her size. When I stand close to her I can see down onto the top of her head. The map, the country, the journey there. We hug and kiss. When I'm in the car with my father and he starts the engine, backing down Tokay into Bricelyn so he can turn around, face down the hill towards Frankstown, she's outside on the porch, wrapped in a trench coat, and as she waves I pretend I can see the white strands, the gray, the wings brushed down on either side of the part running across her skull.

TWO YEARS AGO ON THE WAY TO THE AIRPORT I ASKED my father if he'd like to take a trip to South Carolina sometime. "Sometime" designedly indeterminate as once-upon-a-time, since a journey south with my father, as plan or possibility, had no shape yet in my mind. Just words sounding good inside my head. If I said them aloud, maybe this ride would turn into something less inconclusive than the others.

My father's father, Grandpa to me, had been born near Greenwood, South Carolina. Did I want to go there? Asking myself the question as much as I was testing it on my father. He reminds me he's been to South Carolina twice before: once as a five- or six-year-old and again when he served in the army during World War II.

When I was a kid, my grandfather had attempted to convince me to go south with him. Back to the home place where he was born and raised. Relatives down south still alive then. We'd stay at his sister's house, meet all his siblings who resided around Greenwood forty-odd years ago when Grandpa was offering those summer excursions. I couldn't imagine one good reason for traveling south in those days and plenty for staying put in Pittsburgh. Not that Pittsburgh summers were great, some of the longest days I've ever suffered through occurred during my childhood summers in Pittsburgh. No school, few friends, endless hours to fill, and no ideas or energy or help to fill them. On the other hand, I didn't feature packing off to a place they lynched black boys like Emmett Till for whistling at white women, where you had to move off the sidewalk for crackers to pass, where everybody black was crusty black, and ate watermelon and talked funny. Old, funky people rocking on porches and smoking pipes at night, gone all day picking cotton under the burning sun. No improvement on the city and hotter, and no aunts to spoil me, no department stores or Murphy's five-and-ten or trolley cars. Going to South Carolina was about as appealing as going to Africa and living in the jungle. Only difference between South Carolina and Africa in my mind was the size and variety of the animals. And Africa won that battle. South Carolina had fewer trees and no celebrity like Tarzan swinging through them. In both places the colored people and monkeys too close for comfort. Huh-uh. No thanks, Grandpa. I don't think I want to travel back to slavery days this summer.

Grandpa was persistent. The proposal dusted off each summer, either he'd ask or enlist my mother to pester me. Or both. Grandpa nothing if not stubborn. So was I. A real little iron-headed knucklehead. More than once after my grandfather, Harry Wideman, died in 1978, I've said Thank you and told him how happy I'd be to go, how much I wished he was around to take me. How much I've come to realize I had missed. Said, I'm sorry, Grandpa. You know how kids are. Though it's no compensation for either of us now, I've embarked in my mind on just such a trip countless times.

Imagine it again, riding to the airport with my father. Decide I'm going with him before it's too late again.

Sure. A little vacation would be really nice, my father says. Daddy took me down there when I was a boy. I remember they owned land. Acres and acres. I was little, so you know. Looked like an enormous whole lot of land to me. Pretty green fields. And Daddy's people owned them. He had a gang of brothers. Big men. Big, sturdy men. Picked me up and handled me like a toy. See, I was the first born, Grandpa's son, the first born in the North. Everybody treated me real good. I remember his brothers being tall and powerful-looking. Your grandfather was medium height, but wide, you know, wide. All of them built like him only taller. They couldn't get over Harry's son. Harry's son. As far as I could see in every direction they owned the land. One of Grandpa's sisters, Aunt Annie. That's the name that comes to me. Aunt Annie. She's the one took care of me most the time. Haven't said her name in years. Didn't know I still knew it. Aunt Annie.

Yellow biscuits and white butter. The biscuits yellow down there. No color in the butter. White like lard. Just the opposite of here. I remember being fascinated by that. South Carolina will always be yellow biscuits and white butter to me.

I wandered off and fell into a swamp. Black mud up to my armpits. Hollered and yelled like a little stuck pig. Black mud out behind the house, at the end of one of those pretty green fields. Slipped in and just kept sinking, sinking. Up to my armpits screaming it seemed for the longest damned time before anybody came. Almost drowned in a pool of black muck.

Well, I guess you didn't drown. Somebody must have rescued you cause here you sit. Here I sit.

Uh-huh. But I was in pretty deep. Somebody finally pulled me out. Can't remember who. Bet they were look-

ing everywhere and mad, too. Don't remember a beating.
Daddy seldom hit me. Mommy would have torn me up
if she'd been there. Slipped off when nobody looking and
damn near drowned in a swamp.

That your only time in Greenwood?

Greenwood. Uh-huh. Like I said, during the war I was
stationed in South Carolina. Not Greenwood though.
Greenwood a little town. Our base near a city. A big city
with a humongous harbor. Rows and rows of docks. My
job training a crew how to use heavy equipment to load
and unload ships. Where was it now? Somewhere near
the ocean. A navy base nearby.

Must have been Charleston. Maybe Savannah. But Savannah's Georgia.

Charleston, sure. It was Charleston.

You'd like to go back, then?

Uh-huh. Yes I would.

When?

My social calendar's not overly busy these days, you
know. Especially with this car acting up the way it does.
Afraid to take it anywhere far. I lost a good customer, a
lady I jitneyed way out past Greensburg four mornings a
week to her job. Never missed, but got her there real late
one day. No good. I can't depend on this car, so she
couldn't depend on me. Lost a nice little piece of change.
Think she was getting sweet on your old man, too.
Hmmp. That's the way it goes.

Maybe we'll do it then. I'm on leave next semester so
it won't be so hard to put a week or ten days together.

Yeah. We'll do a roots thing. See if we can find any Widemans down there. See if any old people still around who remember Grandpa.

Have to be pretty old. He'd be over a hundred if he was alive today. And he was a fairly young man, way younger than twenty, I believe, when he left South Carolina for Pittsburgh.

I've been there once. I must have told you. To Promised Land. The little black community outside Greenwood. Read a book about Promised Land, learned Widemans lived there. A Moses Wideman one of the first to buy land on the old Marshall Plantation just after the Civil War. When I was there I discovered plenty of Widemans, but they were all dead. Our name on tombstones in cemeteries. I only had an hour to check out Promised Land. Doing readings and lectures for the South Carolina Humanities Council in schools around the state. Got close to Greenwood and remembered Grandpa's stories, the book. I asked the guy driving me, Steve, Steve Lewis, to make a detour. Saw just enough to whet my appetite for more. Promised Land. Promised myself I'd return some day. Strange. You know. Seeing *Wideman* down there on a gravestone. Who in the world is this with my name under there? Let's do it sometime soon.

You say when. Be more than happy to get out of Pittsburgh awhile. Ready to go when you are, old buddy.

.   .   .

OUR TRIP TO SOUTH CAROLINA STARTED THEN. YOU could look at it that way and then what's transpired in the three years following our conversation is part of the trip. Preparation, so to speak. Or you could treat the intervening years as separate, events conspiring to delay our trip. Or you can try, as I habitually do, to have it both ways and a couple of other ways too, the page being a place like the Australian aborigine's "Dreamtime" where everything happens at once, everything connects, where the function of dream is story and the function of story to create the world. The beginning of the twentieth century's last decade yet plenty of surprises occurring and plenty coming—war pestilence famine flood fire—all part of the trip, as well as the view from my small window while my own first half-century closed down and the twenty-first century hip-hopped to virtual reality in the wings. All part of the trip, but for the moment—for the very good reason we must depart for South Carolina on the date our fourteen-day advance-purchase Saturday-night layover nonrefundable discount tickets stipulate or pay steep penalties—for the moment we forestall stalling, git it on, hit the road, Jack.

AFTER FLYING INTO PITTSBURGH EARLY ON OCTOBER 15 I spend the afternoon and evening at my mother's house, then pick up my father next morning from the Leroy Irvis Towers, a state-subsidized high-rise for the elderly in the Hill District. The Hill not one hill but like much of the city, families of hills climbing and falling all over one another in a rollicking, incestuous sprawl. Downtown, especially at night, a picture postcard from the Irvis homes. Spreading out below the Hill, panoramic views of the city a developer would kill for, the city's center winking and glittering, an enchanted Oz nearly close enough to touch, as distant and inaccessible for the residents of the Irvis Towers as the Milky Way.

From my father's three-by-four-foot balcony I see squadrons of new apartments in various stages of completion where only yesterday vacant lots of urban removal had shingled their way down towards skyscrapers reigning in the city's core. Blocks of brand-new two- and three-story condos form stout fortresses, sealed, separated from bulldozed areas of flattened dwellings. Here and there the odd, truncated row of decayed houses or a solitary building or a gutted shell remain standing. The most polite way to describe this scene of post-apocalypse ruin is to call it a neighborhood in transition.

Once ours, the lower Hill, except for encapsulated clots of public housing, is on the way to becoming theirs. Never really ours in fact. Black people rented here, passed through, or were stuck here, at best owned small pieces of property whose value depreciated to worthless as the projects and private real estate surrounding them were not so much lived in as consumed. People's energies and hungers tax the structures they inhabit. When natural energies and hungers have no healthy outlet, they feed on their hosts, attack friends and family, the physical environment. Destroying what's close, the people they should love and probably do love, the walls, elevators, street lamps, and furniture, the civilized fabric of households, schools, a person sitting on the next bar stool or the guy on his way home from busting dishes in a fast-food joint, the senior citizen who's just cashed a social-security check. What gets torn up is what you can get your hands on.

The poisonous anger at stunted possibilities, the frustration of dying on the vine seep like corrosive acid into living rooms, neighborhoods. Come back at you, source and victim, when you awaken each morning, when you take your first look at where you still are, when you step into the street, when you search for a way out, but *out* is a place hidden inside you where you don't look anymore because it's full of stink and dust, blood and bile.

Black people rented the Hill, tore it up, and moved on. Were moved on. Trekked to what was left of Homewood and East Liberty and Hazelwood and Wilkinsburg, Penn Hills, Garfield, Stanton Heights, wherever we were urban-removed, permitted to settle by white people who controlled what we could buy, where we could buy, how much we had to spend. Moving on Not everybody. The Hill hosted projects, streets not quite demolished, yet so badly mauled time out of mind the residents perhaps hadn't realized their circumstances had gotten worse. Rug pulled out from under them again but no further to fall, nothing to lose. People on the Hill who seemed stoic as roaches, blasé as roaches about blocks condemned, public services canceled, ownership change, zoning changes. You might think the survivors didn't give a fuck unless you looked closer. Not from the height of my father's tenth-floor mini-balcony or from the portholes of condo fortresses. Closer. As close as if your eyes are embedded in the brows of people hanging out of second-story windows, sitting on stoops, scrambling or scurrying or hobbling through the ruins, eyes beset with what Amiri Baraka once called hungers beyond those a white man ever knows.

Since I didn't know the exact location of my father's building, my strategy was driving slowly till I cleared the lower elevations, then emptiness provided an unobstructed view. On one of the last steep shoulders before the land begins its precipitous slide to the jumble of skyscrapers fronting the rivers—Allegheny, Mononga-hela, Ohio—that converge to form the Golden Triangle of the city's heart, the fourteen stories of the Irvis Towers reign. Giant among pygmies, big frog in a little pond, it dwarfs its surroundings. Seeing it the first time, I'd thought less of its dominance than of how cleanly the area beneath it had been picked. Did somebody consciously seek to erect an image of isolation, perversely coordinate all the specs of the building, choose its high ground to smack the observer in the face with thoughts of asylums, prisons, exile. What you see is what you get. In spades.

i thought of K. Leroy Irvis, whose name graces the building. First black speaker of the Pennsylvania House of Representatives, spellbinding orator, master politician, poet, sculptor, dedicated warrior for the right and just as he measured such matters with his great intelligence and

compassion. I'd heard stories about Irvis fighting to de-
segregate public facilities, improve education, reform
prisons, set goals and timetables for equal access and
opportunity from the 1940s till he retired in 1990. A
dogged champion of the predominately black legislative
district he represented, Irvis was also consistently states-
manlike in his determination to keep the larger picture in
sight, honoring the values of enlightened humanism even
as he prevailed with a street fighter's savvy and skill in
the state senate's bruising, daily skirmishes.

Once, decades before, Irvis, serving pro bono as my
father's attorney, had saved his life, and over the years
Irvis's support had been one of the few consistent, bright
spots in a dismal, protracted struggle to have my brother's
life sentence commuted. A giant. A principled man who
couldn't help standing tall in the grinding mediocrity of
state government. As starkly out of scale, as incongru-
ously situated as this hulking building bearing his name.
Beyond that, all comparisons ceased. Associations between the man and building were saturated with irony.

After I'd sighted the building, it was easy to reach.
Supreme in the middle of nowhere, the Irvis Towers was
clearly as much trial as salvation for its old and infirm
residents. Where was the closest store for milk or bread,
let alone a mall? Shopping for daily necessities an expedi-
tion. Long, steep distances in every direction, difficult to
manage in any season, impossible in ice or snow, implacably dangerous for weak hearts and lungs, gimpy legs.
Treacherous in the summer heat, nightmarish after dark,
a windswept barrenness where you could fall and lie for

hours, overnight, unnoticed, except by scavengers who'd rob and strip you, who for sport or evil might set you on fire. Junkies and hoodlums swarmed like bees to honey on the streets around the building the days social-security checks came in. How was a seventy-six-year-old woman supposed to brave this gauntlet of thieves, the changing seasons with their rotating perils. My tough, independent grandfather Harry Wideman wasn't easy to scare, but even he wasn't exempt from the terror. He had described to me the fear tenants experienced each time an elevator door slid open. You never knew what horror might be waiting to trap you, seize you.

Abandoned in an urban wilderness, dealing with the normal portion of depression and loneliness old age can bring, the tenants were also forced to be suspicious, conditioned to avoid and fear the few people outside their building they encountered.

The Irvis Towers was a monument commemorating somebody's good idea, the city's good intentions that wound up exacerbating problems public housing was meant to alleviate.

The entire Hill District, including the scoured, partially rebuilt portion below the Irvis apartments, an answer-in-progress, wasn't it. Tearing down rotten housing, relocating citizens trapped here to other, ideally more wholesome, productive parts of the city. Space cleared for downtown rehabilitation, revitalization, entrepreneurship. The city's core refurbished, the Golden Triangle more radiant than ever, imparting its glow to the entire metropolis.

A seductive idea in the flush post-war fifties that spawned Pittsburgh's Renaissance. Some lives were improved, some areas cleaned up, but many more lives were sacrificed, much damage inflicted on stable if poor and physically unprepossessing black communities. The net result's apparent today: enormous wealth for a few, most of whom began the Renaissance rich; the disease of urban blight that once had been concentrated in a few of the worst places on the Hill and North Side now decentralized, rampant in nearly every black community of the inner city and suburbs. Each area bleeding. Each with its gang turf and drug turf, its chaos of broken homes, broken schools, broken spirits, broken promises, its equal opportunity to participate in the daily shoot-em-ups as young men annihilate themselves in wars whose only purpose seems to be saving their true enemies the trouble of finishing them off. Finishing the destruction of black lives started when the master plan of urban recycling, redistribution of space was conceived.

I've been aware of this history, these circumstances for a long time, if not consciously, then at the back of my neck, where the tiny hairs rise when the body senses danger the mind needs a little bit longer to process. Lots of people share this knowledge. Remember Ralph Ellison's street peddler in *Invisible Man* who earns a living selling carloads of discarded plans and blueprints. Pittsburgh's not unique. Big cities then smaller ones across the country urban-removed, urban-renewed, urban-enhanced themselves and their black populations to death. Plans unraveled. Inner city came to mean sinking ship. Old

plans too costly, too slow, too un-American, too loaded
with welfare handouts to blacks, we were told. The world
changed. Money got tighter. Money better invested
abroad. Or hoarded abroad, etc., etc. The fifties became
the eighties and nineties. The new plan was getting out
of the city as far and as fast as you could. Across the
ocean if you could. Suburbs were ripples expanding at
greater and greater distances from the black hole where
the city was going under, drowning in its own messy
juices. Imploding. Glub. Glub. Down the drain.

But is it really so simple? Perhaps the ranks of nascent
condos, this new phase of slum clearance, embodies a
different message. A new new plan. Sort of.

Oceanfront property is valuable because there will
never be more. What you see is what you get. As population increases, less oceanfront to go around, a shrinking
resource, nearly always a seller's market. What about this
godforsaken, abandoned land below the Irvis Towers?
Was there a larger plan in which it fit, in which its value
might increase? Maybe not any specific person's plan exactly, but a set of conditions like those sustaining, pumping up the price of seashore property.

If you had enough money and patience, city dwellers
would return. The forces that make cities inevitable don't
dry and blow away. Wait for the Hill to depopulate, help
wail-to-wall blackness purge itself, let the urban warfare
burn itself out or divert it, confine it to other regions. At
the point when the land's deserted and dirt cheap, when
you can purchase acres, fields for the cost of square feet
twenty-five years before, buy up the land. Repackage it,

promote it Southern California style. Advertise it as prime real estate. Build islands of neighborhoods, each isolated, demarcated by market forces to achieve the same homogeneity of race and class formal covenants once insured. Watch your investment flourish. Slowly at first, probably too gradual a process for most investors. Only the longest money, the deepest pockets could afford to get in early, but eventually long, long money turns over. Buy cheap, sell dear.

Control of urban space, of black-white relationships as much an incentive as profit. Control, power that might have begun to slip a bit in the sixties, during the Vietnam War, urban insurrections and their aftermath. Fifties-type partnerships between business and government a little too cozy, too transparent, too obviously patriarchal and sexist and racist. Back to the drawing board. Enter the multinational corporation's neutral money. New plans. Play the anxieties of a white middle class against the hopeless spectacle of a black underclass violently self-destructing. Divide and conquer and run up fantastic profits. Then sell the whole mess to the Japanese. Ride off to where you decide the sun should set next before it sets once and for all on the American Empire.

The sale of abandoned public housing to private speculators a mini-drama, a test case, a kind of Spanish civil war dress rehearsal and preview of grander possibilities.

Fortunes are being amassed by investors who purchase for a song the bad idea of public housing. These investors buy uninhabitable, crime-infested warrens from the government, clean them up, institute new management policies unencumbered by state and federal regulations intended to protect tenants who occupy public housing. Draconian sweeps dislodge undesirables. Private cops maintain order. Low purchase costs, tax breaks, quick resale produce huge profits. These retooled projects no longer serve the segment of the population, the poor, for whose benefit public monies originally had been allotted. Taxpayers' money that had financed construction and subsidized rent becomes a subsidy for private investors. Streamlined and steamrolled into the streets, the poor once more are displaced, find themselves eating somebody's bad plan, a new plan eating them. The *haves* profit from yet another pressing of the *have-nots*.

Consider the post–Rodney King scorched earth of South Central Los Angeles as another version of urban removal. Who was responsible for the riot/rebellion/ethnic cleansing? Who lost, who stands to profit?

MY FATHER, SUITCASE IN HAND, IS OUT OF THE TIGHTLY secured Irvis Towers before I can ring the front doorbell to get in. I'm still fumbling, not with an economic analysis in which, intentionally or not, greed and genocide are two sides of the same coin, but with the unfamiliar keys and locks of a rental car that will take us to the Greater Pittsburgh Airport. He'd told me on the phone his car had been stolen from the lot. His car wasn't worth much. Probably ripped off for parts, sitting now in a vacant lot or alley, stripped down, growing rust. Plenty of nicer cars the thieves could have chosen. My father feels he's been unfairly singled out and that rankles him nearly as much as his loss. He couldn't afford theft insurance. A year's premium more than the car's worth. Of course the vehicle's value to him went far beyond the book price. A car's the difference between walking and riding, and walking, when you're stuck in this high-rise, amounts to wearing a leash around your neck, a thirty-pound ball on your shoulder.

He's managing okay, he says. Buses. Jitneys. Footmobile. He'll make do. Raggedy as it was, though, he misses his Custom Cruiser. Somebody comes Sundays to take him and his sister, my Aunt Catherine, who also lives in the building, to church. But you need a car here. Don't know why they stole mine. Look around. Some nice-looking rides. I'd be scared to park a really good car out here. Thugs would have it and gone in a minute.

U.S. Air flight 179 from Pittsburgh to Charlotte, North Carolina. Rental car for the drive on Interstate 85 from Charlotte to Greenville, South Carolina. Route 25 Greenville to Greenwood, South Carolina. Pretty straightforward. A total of 150 miles from Charlotte to Greenwood, a chance to see the countryside.

The shape of South Carolina reminds me of Africa, only stumpier, foreshortened, the graceful, gradually tapering tail of the continent is missing. A broad-shouldered triangle, one long side, defined by the Savannah River, borders Georgia. A sort of humpbacked, stair-stepped northern boundary abuts North Carolina and Tennessee. The shortest side seacoast with its ports, sea islands, low-lying littoral perfect for the cultivation of rice. Rivers, creeks, lakes, ocean, all baby blue in my atlas. You're never too far from water in South Carolina. The capital, Columbia, more or less in the center of the state. Colored lavender on my map with yellow and black shields bearing their numbers, interstate highways intersecting at Columbia are Xs carved across the face of the state.

South Carolina, the heart of the Confederacy. Local historians claim Abbeville as the heart of that heart, say the Confederacy was born and died there—a mass meeting on Abbeville's Succession Hill, November 22, 1860, led to South Carolina becoming the first state to secede from the Union; President Jefferson Davis, fleeing from the Union Army, convened the last official meeting with his cabinet and war council May 2, 1865, in a mansion just outside the town.

In the outline of South Carolina you can see that Valentine heart shape, but a heart violently mutilated, one chamber karate-chopped so its soft arc is missing.

A spinning top or heart or wedge or crooked arrowhead or keystone, you can name the triangular form whatever you wish. Treat it as a mirror, search for your face.

We're heading down Route 25, nearing Greenwood, looking for signs to Promised Land, when I spot a cutoff for Abbeville. I seem to recall stopping in Abbeville on my previous trip, examining ledgers in Abbeville Courthouse, being advised a fire had destroyed most of the older records. The memory's dreamlike. Mixed with images of wooden buildings burning, the crackle of walls, pages consumed. Whether or not I'd actually stopped there before, the city had worked its way inside me. It would be déjà vu when we arrived this time. Promised Land is not on my map. For some reason I think going to Abbeville will get us closer to Promised Land. Or perhaps the reason for going in that direction is a sound and its associations. Something Old World, mysterious, medieval, monkish, flying buttresses, crenellated steeples, in the town's name. Or perhaps it's not the name as much as it is the simple attraction of foreplay. According to my calculations, if we're only twelve miles from Greenwood, we've almost reached Promised Land. I don't want to arrive at our destination too soon, too easily. Don't want the weight of what to do next on my mind quite yet.

I tell my father I'm not sure whether the turnoff to Abbeville is a shortcut or detour. Either way, he says, fine with him. We've been in the rental car over two hours, my back's aching from a mushy car seat constructed in the American fashion to swallow not support. The fragile last inch or so of the string that connects my spine to my backside registers with a hot jolt of pain every minute pull upward of my steepled knees, every shift of my butt pulling down. My father's a large man and twenty years older so he can't be very comfortable either. I'm hoping Abbeville is worth the trouble, won't add too much extra time.

Already we've set a record. Departed from the parking lot of the Irvis Towers around 7:00 A.M. About 2:30 P.M. as we turned off Route 25 towards Abbeville. Over seven hours together. Unless he'd watched me for longer than that when I was a baby, I'd never spent this much time alone with my father. Seven hours and counting. Or not counting anymore. Which was better. Better to lose track, to stop counting. I wanted our time together to be simple, relaxed, ordinary. One mistake had been treating my father as if a father always required a capital F. As long as I carried a deity, a natural force in my mind, I wouldn't see the man on the seat beside me. Why had it been impossible all these years to believe in this man's actual life, him with a suitcase in his hand, excited, anxious to get the hell away from the everyday tedium of growing old, alone and poor.

SOME FACTS I RECALL ABOUT MY FATHER, THINKING about him, thinking about writing about him on this November afternoon three years after our trip to Promised Land. He shadowboxed; was a soldier in World War II, guarded Japanese prisoners of war on Saipan; made us stand when "The Star-Spangled Banner" played on the radio; born in Pittsburgh, Pennsylvania; moved to Washington, D.C., with my mother in 1941 to work in a government printing office; one sister, Catherine—living; one brother, Eugene—killed in Guam by a sniper in 1945. My father played all sports well. When he was one of the "older" guys, he competed against future NBA pros Charlie Cooper, Maurice Stokes, and Ed Fleming on the basketball court in Westinghouse Park beside the swimming pool in Homewood. He once defended himself with his knife against a man who attacked him with a knife; raised one set of children (me and four siblings) with my mother; fathered at least one other set, and a son about my age, upon women he never married; worked as a waiter at Kaufmann's Department Store in downtown Pittsburgh; worked as a welder at Dravo shipyards; rooted for the New York Yankees; liked to mix his Scotch with milk, liked Canadian whiskey; a voracious reader of pulp westerns; attended University of Pittsburgh for a brief time on GI benefits; speaks precise, uninflected English, colored more by Pittsburghisms (you *rid up* rooms, not "clean" them) than African-American markers; nicknamed "Sweetman" by his fellow garbagemen during the years he worked for the city as a "sanitary engineer"; often fell asleep in his chair at family gatherings or the end of the evening at home.

Is distance, the difference between us, simply a matter of questions not asked? If I add items to the list of things I can recall about my father, will they answer questions or raise questions? Will they bring us closer to Promised Land? Or will it always be just down the road a piece? *Fatheralong.*

Fatheralong

PERHAPS IT'S INEVITABLE. THE HAIRLINE RECEDING, THE stone rolled back, the need to peer into the tomb of what's happened and yet to happen, to imagine yourself entering then returning, the conversations you might have had with your father, if he could have spoken, if you had been ready to listen to whatever he might have said. My friend Mike nods his head. Boy. I wish I had the chance now, you know. He says the words slowly, pauses between words, staring away from me into the emptiness shrouding his dead father when I tell him I'm thinking about traveling to Pittsburgh then South Carolina for the long-delayed conversations with mine.

Age brings you to your father. You are much older now than he was in your earliest memory of him, old enough to be the father of the man he was that day in Pittsburgh, snow falling, the downtown sidewalks crowded with parade watchers, your father a young man lifting you to his shoulder so you peer over other people's heads into the cleared space where the marchers will appear, a space yawning and vacant and unaccountably frightening, it would swallow you, you'd sizzle and disappear like a water drop in a hot skillet if you stepped out there. You cannot fathom how this broad, empty avenue you wouldn't dare cross will bear the weight of everything you expect to fill it any second, contain the parade you've been waiting hours for, the memory of it ancient before it arrives.

You recall snow and it may have been snowing that cold afternoon in Pittsburgh waiting for a parade, but none of it sticks, it dissolves as swiftly on the streets as it does when you tilt your face up to find the snow's source. When you think no one is looking, you open your mouth, sneak out your tongue, and the nothing taste of snow disappoints you, another wet blot barely lasts long enough on your eyelash to flick away.

Snow seems part of that afternoon, falling perhaps early in the day and stopping before the parade commences, or a damp raw chill in the air the whole time you are standing watching, then flurries gradually more visible until the parade's scraggly tail end approaches, then larger and larger white flakes swirl around the marchers, the spectators, flakes beginning to settle, to cover the streets of the parade route, the entire downtown disappearing under a blanket of whiteness, everything quiet and gone without a trace as the trolley you ride with your mother carries you through darkening streets home.

Snow part of the earliest memory of my father whether it was falling that day or not, snow frames the picture, a stylized presence at the edges, a curtain I brush aside to enter, a silence shutting again behind my back as I depart, snow and the certainty I am wrapped in many layers of clothes, my mother would have overdressed me for the winter day and trip downtown, the normal gravity of how it felt to stand with my own two feet on the sidewalk absent. Boots, snowsuit, mittens sweater flannel shirt bibbed corduroy trousers undershirt two pairs of socks a cap hood and scarf muffled me, bloated me, made me an astronaut long before anybody had walked on the moon, a deep-sea diver just this side of the bends after my father snatches me from the ocean floor to the promontory of his shoulder. I believe snow fell that day and know I was dressed for the Arctic. Know I snuggled up to my mother and slept during the long trolley ride home from downtown, though my only proof of these things is this memory of snow the day I'm constructing almost fifty years later, letting pieces float into place as I know they must have, tilting my head back again to find the hole in the sky where everything comes from.

I know my father is not on the trolley my mother and I ride home from the Thanksgiving Day parade. I'm asleep, tired from the long, full day that started for me before dawn, lying awake listening for the first sounds of my mother up. The room still dark as I drift free of sleep, anticipating her bare feet slapping the floor, her trip to pee, imagining what the day might bring, exhausting myself trying to name things that might happen, wanting to be asleep again so I could hurry up and wake up again in the middle of everybody's preparations to go. The kind of restless, excited morning alone in bed remembering times when all I'd need to drop peacefully asleep would be my mother's body, her warmth, the sound and smell of her, her hand stroking my hair, folding me closer into her sleep, a sleep she doesn't need to break to let me in. Tired long before the day started for anyone else so I lean into her, drift, melt, the charmed circle of her arm around my shoulders hugging me while the trolley sways and clomps like the old ice-wagon horse over broken streets.

My father would not be on the trolley because he goes on to another job after his downtown-morning-till-late-afternoon gig in the restaurant of Kaufmann's Department Store. I visited him once on the top floor of Kaufmann's, waiting for hours it seemed, anxious to be noticed and not noticed, till one of the brown men in white jackets asked me if I was Eddie's son and smiled at me when I nodded and mumbled Yessir. He said, Just a minute, sonny, you sit down right here just a minute. I'll fetch your daddy. My father's buddy Chooky, Chooky Bolden whose name I wouldn't have heard for years until my mother said it to someone, "poor man drank himself to death, passed out and froze to death in his own driveway." Chooky Bolden snatched the used white cloth from the table where he'd seated me, folding it while it still floated in the air, tucking it under one arm as he produced another from somewhere and unfurled it, whiter, brighter, snapping it like a shoeshine rag so it spread and hovered a split second before settling over the round tabletop. With more hands than anyone I'd ever seen, he continued doing three or four things simultaneously. In an instant plates, saucers, cups, glasses, silverware, salt and pepper shakers, menus, and napkins red as the restaurant rug were arranged before me. Eddie be here soon as he can. Been busy as a bee's nest in here. Bout got it whipped now. Crackers be clearing out lickety-split. How you doing today, sonny? You're a fine-looking young man. Look just like your daddy. Said all at once and too quickly for me to reply even if I'd known what I was supposed to say back to the brown-skinned man in his black pants and gleaming white jacket who was gone before I could be sure he'd been standing there in front of me, loading and unloading the skinny cart he wheeled away before I could open my mouth. Or shut it. Chooky Bolden who took our orders, served my father and me in our corner of a restaurant of white people with a kind of seamless efficiency, always present but unseen till we need something, there and not there, invisible as I hoped we were to the other diners, invisible as they were to me from our corner table because I kept my eyes on my plate or on my father's face the whole time we ate. Pretending the white people weren't there was a way of keeping them from bothering us, protecting the precious, private time with my father.

Having lunch with me at a white-topped table served

by Chooky Bolden was not my father's job. I was afraid they'd summon him away any minute to do his job, and I'd be left alone. If I could have, I would have held on to some part of him the whole time, wrist or ankle or hooked my arm around his neck. But he was not in the trolley. In addition to waiting tables at Kaufmann's he worked at two different clubs Monday through Thursday and many private parties weekends. I couldn't keep up with where he was nights or which hours he was supposed to be home. I just knew better than to bother him because he might be asleep any hour of the day.

Five days a week, roughly during school hours, if I thought of my father, I could place him in the dining room of Kaufmann's Department Store. After my visit I could place myself there also, keeping out of people's way, avoiding the eyes of anybody who might ask me my business, ask me what business did I have hanging around a restaurant only grown white people entered and left, what business did I have slipping past the hostess and the little brass pole with a tasseled rope attached she lowered and raised to regulate traffic. At my desk in school I could see myself spying on the waiters in short white jackets and black pants, needing one to be my father, trying to guess which one, afraid my father's face, like mine when I ventured into unknown places, might change. He'd be wearing different features when he waited tables at Kaufmann's and I'd never find him.

So I did not expect him to ride the trolley home with us from the parade. I didn't expect him to do much more than come and go like a ghost, at odd hours, to sleep, to eat, to meet me that one time on his job when I stepped off the elevator to have lunch with him and go to a movie, the two of us alone for once. He was my father and worked long and hard for us. We slept in the same house but at different hours. He was around or not around according to a schedule I couldn't fathom but believed unfair. I learned to accept things as they were, not to expect more, learned as kids must, the only way around powerlessness is to make up stuff, to cheat, steal, lie.

In the house on Copeland Street in Shadyside we lived on the second floor. My mother and father slept in a closet-sized room at the end of the hall on the landing above the front-door stairs. With no particular reason to be sneaky, other than I definitely didn't want anyone else to know what I was doing, I'd stand in my parents' room when it was empty or sit in the hall outside their door those odd weekend daylight times when the rest of us were up but my father still inside the room snoring away.

Why these were secret times, times I felt vaguely ashamed of then and still do, I can't exactly say. Perhaps the secret had something to do with my father's smell, seeping off his body while he slept, in his clothes, the sheets and blankets when he wasn't in the room. A smell inseparable from the fact he was larger, stronger, darker, that he occupied lots of space, owned it, stamped it even when he wasn't around. Not stink exactly, but the funk of maleness, his work, his sweat and breathing, his comings and goings when the rest of us weren't awake, him staying out all night if he wanted to, or sleeping all day, his power to leave the house, to raise his voice and punish us whether we deserved it or not, to fill the room, the bed he shared with my mother, to shit and shave first in the bathroom, singing while the rest of us waited, scuffling Sunday mornings to get ready for church. Not exactly stink but a threat of nastiness in the scent he marked things with. Pungent nastiness I envied and feared because it defined something about my person too, something he'd pass on to me, the sign of myself clinging to me as his clings to him, a cause when I was around other people of deep shame and embarrassment, a source when I was alone of bottomless curiosity.

I breathed him in and it was like stealing, like unwrapping an edge of one of those silver-foil packets he brought home from jobs and pinching nibbles from the delicacies whose names I didn't know, often didn't like the salty taste of, but needed to pry open and sample anyway, even at the risk of my father's wrath, trespassing perhaps because I wanted to get caught, wanted to trigger my father's anger, the real thing when he'd snatch me or shake me or yell at me then fix me in a glare that said, Boy, something awful's going to happen to you, happen with no mercy, no escape, so terrible I need a minute to figure out just how I'm going to arrange it. Maybe what I hoped to get when I dug into the booty he liberated from the fancy parties he served was a taste of him, even if it had to take the form of an angry exchange, it would be preferable to opening the refrigerator and finding the shiny package gone. Preferable to waiting for the other kind of anger, trumped-up, secondhand, when he was less mad at me than at my mother for setting him up to be the executioner after he dragged in from work because I'd acted up during the day and she'd laid down the wait-till-your-father-gets-home threat for him to make good and he has to tighten his lips and coax the chill into his eyes and hurt me enough so I swear I'll never do it again, never do it again.

Learning his odor, fixing it in my mind, the same way I made it my business to bumble around with every sense hyper-alert in rooms in my grandmother's house on Finance Street where women were dressing or undressing or relaxing, not dressed in much at all, me not seeming to pay any attention to them and too young anyway, they thought, to be thinking much about the parts of them different than my parts. Sometimes one of my aunts or my mother would call me over, smile, pat me on the head, and I'd see bare breasts or brush against something soft or naked it would take me years to see again or touch again on some other live female body, some other soft sweet tune playing for me in love or not in love in a different fashion with the bare flesh I touched or watched later. A different kind of intimacy years later but also returning me to the wonder and bonding of those early, easy times with my aunts and mother when I was a spy, a fly on the wall of warm, scented rooms in which they dressed and undressed, chatting with each other, casual in their bodies, unsuspicious or not caring or benignly silent about everything bad they understood about me better than I knew myself, letting me disappear as they busied themselves with the things women do together, do alone.

On the trolley my mother's saying something to me but I hear only singsong nicknames, baby prattle, nothing in her voice I can't draw down with me into the place where I'm pretending not to be awake. She's fishing for me with little bright bobbing teasing lures, coaxing me out of the deep pocket of her where I'm hiding. C'mon you. I know you're not asleep. She's not playing now, not singing. I can not remember precisely how, but I could tell from the feel of the trolley when we had arrived in Homewood. I knew, even though I possessed no words then or now to say it precisely, how riding a trolley through Homewood was different than riding it anywhere else. You'd know even if you were blind. The side-to-side pitch or jolts, the rhythm of stop and go. You wouldn't need eyes to see the Homewood people, the Homewood buildings, or ears to hear Homewood voices. Riding along with your eyes squeezed shut and hands over your ears you could feel the steep inclines, the sharp curves, a long smooth glide at the bend of Frankstown Avenue, Hamilton's cobblestones chattering your teeth. So I knew why my mother had stopped singing. Why she pulled away so I had to balance myself upright on the trolley seat's hard weave. My own backbone and backside responsible again inside the bundle of clothes she'd made me wear to the parade. We were home again.

The walk from the trolley stop on Hamilton Avenue to my grandmother's house on Finance Street is not far, only five or six short blocks, but also for years much farther than I was allowed to venture on my own. So that evening, after the parade, and nights years later when I'm out prowling for women or mischief or both and cross Hamilton, it registered as a boundary, a line dividing my turf from unknown territory. Walking, probably with my hand in my mother's, through dark, empty, snow-dusted streets from the trolley stop home the night of the parade I knew exactly what was waiting for me. The streets were like the bulky clothing I wore, not me, maybe even a little cumbersome, unnecessary, but I felt comfortable and protected inside them and understood that in a few minutes I'd be free of them, home, relaxing, getting ready for bed. The same short passage, the same walk on Dunfermline past the same houses and trees and street corners, changed if you were going from Finance to Hamilton, the opposite direction, away from home rather than towards home. Then you were approaching the edge, you didn't wear the streets, they rode your back, giddy-up, go, go, go on, boy, urging you to cross Hamilton and get into whatever was over there, what wasn't tamed or predictable, whatever made those streets, those rungs climbing the ladder of Bruston Hill—Kelly, Sterrett, Braddock, Frankstown—different and forbidden till you were grown enough to know better, or think you did, and not give a good goddamn.

Beyond Hamilton you might run into your father. I wouldn't have thought that then. But my mother did, her sisters and her mother did, so somehow the knowledge must have been part of me, learned as I learned most things, not only because of what the women said, but because I also studied the school of their bodies, how they moved, their silences, the animation of hands and lips and eyes, touching, guiding, freeing my flesh. They practiced on me as if I could be all the men they'd ever known or wished they'd known or cared to know: Don't you wish his granddaddy was here today to see him. Daddy'd be so proud, he'd bust a gut. This boy's his father all over again. Look at those bedroom eyes. Trouble for some poor gal someday. I'm glad he got at least a taste of his father's color. Nothing more handsome than a good-looking dark brown-skinned man. Horton's color. Yes, indeed. Horton Moon was a handsome dog in his day. Still is if he'd stop wearing that Afro wig. More dog than handsome in that black, good-for-nothing nigger. Made me so mad sometimes I could wring his neck. Whoa. If he drove up today in that three-tone green Buick Riviera and tooted his horn, you'd knock us down, girl, getting out to the curb. I'd tell you something else knock you down if Mr. Bigears wasn't sitting over in the corner taking everything in. And then Aunt Catherine Moon would cut her eyes and do something with one shoulder, shrugging something off or pumping herself up or hinting at some dance move memorized long ago and buried deep in nerves and muscles, a slight hitch, twitch, jerk, snap, dip of one shoulder releases her entire body, lightens her, raises her on her toes so whatever else she's doing, wherever she happens to be, she is also for a sixteenth of a second twenty-one years old again and dancing in the South Park Pavilion to Jeeps Blues. Or the gesture means something else entirely I can only guess at, amazed how the mystery both unravels and deepens. Will the same gesture another time, another place, another woman performing it, teach me more? Whatever it meant, she felt better after doing it and I loved it and it registered as a whole story about Aunt Catherine, my father's sister. She was okay, all right, fine, no matter what foolishness or hurt came before or followed the gesture. She was fine. Flashed her power then locked it up again with those other resources she could bring to bear on what might be unmanageable otherwise.

If I sensed I might run into my father, over there in the disreputable, darker streets of Homewood, then crossing Hamilton must have been a way of seeking him. Not his person, but all the power and privilege I associated with his person. Built into the seeking were also many levels of betrayal. I was betraying the women who lived in my grandmother's house on Finance, the confidences they'd shared with me, their confidence in me. What in the world could I be looking for across Hamilton, except the precise dangers the women had organized their lives, with great cost to themselves, to protect me from. Painstakingly organized their dress and speech, their manner of comporting themselves in public, organized their church, its music and prayers and Sunday school and upright deacons, who'd managed like the women in my family to stay off the far end of Homewood Avenue, the nastiness flourishing there we'd see the tail of sometimes as it straggled up past the church from Hamilton Avenue, unwashed, shameless, high as a kite, loud and

oblivious on a Sunday morning. Like it was any old morning. Pointing, teasing, laughing at us dressed in our Sunday best as we're hustled into the church's side door by
some scandalized, fit-to-be-tied adult. I could toss all the
women's sacrifices out the window simply by putting my
foot on the wrong path at the wrong time. Once. Betrayal
was loss of respect for them, their struggle on my behalf,
the one they'd died for a little bit, to raise a little bit
higher, the one into whose hands they'd chanced so
much of themselves that disrespecting myself would also
be bringing them down.

Did the prospect of finding my father over there beyond Hamilton put my flight in a different light? Not so
much deserting or shaming the women, as it was seeking
him. Loyalty the flip side of betrayal. If and when I found
him, would he punish me for being in the wrong place,
doing the wrong thing, punish me or welcome me or
instruct me how to run farther, how to find my way home
again.

Whatever I caught him doing or he caught me doing
in the bars or poolroom or sitting on the porch steps of
a houseful of pretty women or standing on the corner
working out schemes to get off the goddamn same ole
shit corner, schemes you couldn't forge or discuss anywhere except on the corner and therefore schemes keeping your ass nailed to the corner day after day working
out details, wherever we bumped into each other I hoped
the flash of light when he recognized and spoke to me
would be bright enough, the music loud enough to drown
the sound of walls tumbling, the women shaking their

heads and dropping their eyes in embarrassment and disappointment. Lost in some joint in Frankstown where I'd dragged them to look for my daddy.

Betraying him, too. Because seeking him in the bars, the streets over there beyond Hamilton, I was confirming the women's version of him. Searching for proof, trying to catch him red-handed. The part of me that was him, part of the evidence against him. My guilt proved his, his proved mine. Out there carrying on just like your father. Tattletale proof in the pudding.

On the other hand, there was always the chance I might learn something new, something the women neglected to tell me, didn't know, couldn't know since they'd never hung out in the places where my father went nights. Maybe I could bring back glad tidings. Maybe I could come and go between my mother's world and my father's world, close the gap separating them.

But a spy couldn't be an emissary, couldn't pretend to be a proper spy until he figured out whom he was serving, where his loyalties finally resided, and that question was irresolvable, remains so this instant.

The first rule of my father's world is that you stand alone. Alone, alone, alone. A fact about which we have no choice or say, carved in stone above the portal we enter when we arrive on this earth. Your work in the world is to grasp this truth, never lose sight of it, turn it so it catches light from all angles, squeeze it till its hardness, its intractability is alchemied into a source of strength. Accept the bottom line, icy clarity of the one thing you can rely on: nothing. Your power, your work is to exempt yourself from illusion, handle yourself, conduct your business without ever forgetting who and what you can count on: nothing. You are proud when you don't let yourself forget and always wind up regretting your slips, those occasions when you compromise, when you let go of the truth even for a second, even in the smallest exchanges with the few people you allow a smidgen closer to you than you allow everyone else. You are, if you're my father, calculating, relentless, disciplined beyond belief in adhering to this self-imposed regimen. Not because it brings happiness or satisfaction in the usual sense. You don't expect to make things better. You don't do what you do in order to produce consequences anywhere but within your own skull, on the meter toting up your hardheaded power to deny, to withdraw, to remain detached. What counts is the doing, the discipline, the engagement with nothing on its own terms.

My mother's first rule was love. She refused to believe she was alone. *Be not dismayed, whate'er betides/God will take care of you.* The nothing my father acknowledged was for her just as cold and hard and unbearable a truth, but it could not encroach beyond a circle she drew in the air around herself. Her God's arms were that circle and he was also inside with her. Think of circling arms. My mother's arms around her children, her grandkids, her sisters and brother, nephews and nieces, and inside that circle of family, smaller circles, two bodies clinging, five or six in a tight huddle, circles concentric, overlapping, intertwined, generations long gone and yet to be born connected indivisibly. The first circle a pinpoint of affection gleaming in a child's eye, the last a radiant, all-encompassing arc, the great mother or great father's embrace. Unbroken circles expanding, contracting, rainbow circles you can visualize an instant if you don the mask of Damballah, hold all time, Great Time in your unflinching gaze.

Think of thread spun finer than silk but steel-strong, stronger, much stronger as it stretches, loops, weaves, webs. The yawning void, nothingness stopped outside the ring of love. A fingertip pressing against yours with the resolution, the determination not to lose touch becomes a fence against the nothing.

Love the work, love the power in my mother's world. You are not alone unless you let go of love, and if you let go, then you truly are nothing.

I couldn't maintain a foot in both worlds. The stretch was too great. Neither Father's son nor Mother's son, betraying them both as I became myself. My mother's open arms. My father's arms crossed on his chest.

IN MY GRANDMOTHER'S HOUSE ON FINANCE STREET the night of the Thanksgiving Day parade, a ritual enacted as it was every other night. All right now. Time to go. Say your prayers now and go to sleep. Sometimes I'd slide down to my knees on the floor beside the bed, fold my hands, bow my head, and recite the singsong rhymes. On cold nights if I'd already slipped beneath the covers, peaceful and content, drifting seamlessly from our quiet time to sleep, my mother would say, Don't forget your prayers. I'd chant them curled on my side or lying flat on my back so I could stare at the darkness gathering below the ceiling, a darkness tame and quiet as long as my mother remained in the room, as long as the prayer words in my mouth and the door cracked to catch the yellow glow from the hall. I could think about darkness calmly, address questions to it until I said good night and my mother said good night and love you and the last light drained from the room as she closed the door behind her. Some nights she'd say, Whoa. What's your hurry, young man? Not so fast. Say every word clearly. When you pray God listens to you. Every word. And don't forget to put Aunt Fanny in your prayers tonight.

My father was never in the room but always in the prayer, in his spot close to the end of the line of bless this one and bless that one finishing my prayers each night. *God bless Mommy and Daddy and everybody in the whole wide world amen.* If my mother didn't slow me down, I'd turn the prayer into one long word, like the pledgeallegiancetotheflag and Our Father Who Art in Heaven became once I'd started school and repeated them every morning, standing with hand over heart for one, then sitting head bowed mumbling the other into my desk. One long string of nonsense syllables inflected, modulated so they sound vaguely the way words would, swept up in a chorus of other voices, chanted *da-da, da-da, da dum-dum da*, music for my mother's ears as I knelt in the quiet room, the quiet house where black night would begin grunting, mumbling unspeakable threats as soon as the door closed behind my mother.

Now I lay me down to sleep . . . then the rest that never
varied, till the end. Then the list of *God blesses*, beginning
with my mother and father, including an extra name
when I was prompted by my mother, and eventually
stretched to fit my siblings, added one by one, a crowd
of names inserted at the prayer's tail end, latecomers
butting in even here, in the private time with my mother
before sleep. My father too, a kind of intruder, there and
not there. I didn't exactly think of him when I asked God
to bless *Daddy*. Although I've called my father "Daddy"
all my life, still do, *Daddy* is a neutral word, doesn't stir
up much of anything, so it was just one of the appropriate
sounds I'd run together into *la-di-da* music pleasing my
mother, rounding day into night. My father not really
there and I'm pretty sure I didn't want him there, no more
than I wanted my sister and brothers there, at least no
more of him than the biff-bam-thank-you-ma'am glimmer
of someone real who scarcely appears in a dim doorway
before the door slams, he's gone, the beat rolls on.

"Our Father," the first words in the school prayer. That
Father not mine either. The faces of God, of Jesus were
white faces with silky flowing hair and flowing beards.
Like other white people they spoke strangely and you
learned you were supposed to be careful around them,
address them in peculiar ways. None of that had much to
do with my father's face. The *Daddy* I blessed, the *Father*
in the Lord's Prayer, were words said aloud, about someone absent. Words pushing me to imagine other places,
an elsewhere, distant, unfamiliar, even frightening, since
to place myself where the words resided, I would need to

let go of what was solid, dependable, the tangible texture of what made me, for better or worse, who I was. I think we rushed through the pledge and prayer at school because we understood they demanded more of us than we were prepared to relinquish. Imagining my father, attaching a name to the little I understood about him, to the vastness I intuited but couldn't grasp, was too much for me to ask of myself. He dwelt out there, elsewhere, wherever, and maybe that was the best place for him to remain.

I THINK I'M BEGINNING TO DISCOVER AS I SHUFFLE through childhood memories of my father, not so much recollecting as reexperiencing them, something of a paradox. I was of his flesh, fashioned in his image. Everybody said I looked just like him, but it was my body, the mirror of him, estranging me most from him. The ways I learned my body. The secret, inner life growing as my body grew.

For a long time, from birth and before, my body belonged to the women in my family. It was the sum of the intimacies they lavished on me. Hugged and bathed and tucked in a warm bed, rocked on a knee, pressed to a bosom, snuggled in a lap. They cared for me; I was totally comfortable only with them. They taught me my body's alphabet, taught it to speak and listen. Often my body would merge with my mother's or with one of her sisters who lived with us in my grandmother's house. Cuddled up for a nap or occasionally sleeping all night beside a woman sleeping, the intimacy of merging was also an exploration of difference. Learning boundaries, places I could touch and not touch, places where the women's bodies changed, attracting me, scaring me, where they became so unlike me I could not decipher the mystery of difference solely with my senses. I needed more than the creature-to-creature rubbing and sniffing and listening intimacies a child was permitted. If my eyes, ears, nose, fingertips, and toes couldn't explain difference, perhaps daydreaming would. I believe it's at this juncture my father materialized. As soon as I began to stand apart, ponder and worry the power of women's bodies, he stepped into the room. Not in the flesh, the flesh we shared, but as an absence, someone like me who would know exactly what I was up to, peeking, sneaking around. Wasn't I on my way to being him?

In the room full of women's secrets I birthed him; the idea of him, a man, a father, allowed me to be in the room but also elsewhere, thinking about the room, perhaps visualizing it as he might. Didn't I need a father to explain my bewilderment, my desire, the hidden part of me that spied and calculated, the predatory part I hadn't been aware of until differences between the women's bodies and mine created space, curiosity, the compulsion to verify and simultaneously remove what separated me from them?

I learned the differences between women's bodies and mine couldn't be willed away, even with a father's help. Difference created guilt, pleasure, and pain. If my father knew my secrets, if we shared them, would he punish me? Or understand and welcome me. Did my ambivalence about what I was doing, what I was becoming, anger me as I grew away from the women? Did I blame my father? His presence, his absence. Wanting him gone, missing him so much, I imagined him as a kind of deity, all power in his hands, confused him with God because he bore God's names, because God was up in the sky, far away, invisible, and didn't the women, my mother and her sisters, love him?

One evening, during one of those rare dinnertimes my father wasn't working and the family could sit down together for a meal, my mother told some tale on me and my father laughed and called me a knucklehead or one of his other words for little-black-sambo dumbness. I was feeling feisty, reading lots of Edgar Rice Burroughs's Tarzan books, picking up a vocabulary of hunting, tracking terms, lore about jungle flora and fauna, a casebook of examples illustrating how the superior intelligence, courage, and civilization of a lone white man enabled and entitled him to achieve dominion over all God's creatures, including the savage, ignorant, black natives he found himself stranded among in Africa, natives beneath my contempt as I turned pages and swung with Tarzan through the treetops. So I didn't appreciate that knucklehead-sambo shit and snapped back at my father.

Well, you're a spoor.

What did you call me?

Spoor.

Pow. He smacked me across my face. My father's hands boxer quick. I never saw the blow coming. Heard it before I felt it. A red blur, one whole side of my face on fire. Burning from shame as much as pain. The crimson color inside my skin suddenly exploding outside, turning the world blood red as I squinted through hot mist. My cheek stung but the smack hadn't been intended to hurt as much as humiliate. The loud, openhanded, sudden impact of a cherry bomb booming in the middle of this quiet family dinner of meatloaf, peas, mashed potatoes, and gravy. I was the eldest. The younger kids seldom saw me punished. If they ever did and I caught them looking, they knew they'd catch double or quadruple what I'd caught. But here we sat around the kitchen table and our father had smacked me in the face and no way I could perpetrate on them the shock of what they'd witnessed happening to me.

With everyone's eyes and ears focused on me I couldn't cry. If he'd knocked me down or out, it would have been better. Out cold on the floor I wouldn't be burdened with inventing a response and everybody would have taken my side. The younger kids would be bawling, my mother rushing to rescue me. Oh my God. Have you gone insane? Are you hurt, baby?

I'm sure I raised my hand to my blazing cheek, probably both hands up to hide my face, give myself time to compose a mask. *Why, why, why* ringing in my ears.

The outraged innocence and indignation of those whys disintegrated as quickly as the ringing from the blow. Behind the screen I instantly began to plot my revenge. There couldn't be a reason why. My father was bigger, stronger, and bullies don't need reasons for bullying. *Spoor*. He probably doesn't know what the word means. He's mad cause he doesn't know cause spoor is worse than knucklehead cause I'm smarter already and he knows it. I beat him and that's why. I scored on him and all a bully can do is retaliate like a bully, reach across the dinner table and *pow*, knock me upside the head.

Who do you think you're talking to, boy?

I hoarded the glare that was a perfect answer to his question behind my hands. When I raised my head, the expression on my face told everybody I was a stranger just passing through the neighborhood and didn't have a clue about what might be transpiring in this obscure kitchen. Dry-eyed I stared blankly at a spot midway between the ceiling and the top of the head of the tallest person sitting at the table.

Look at me when I speak to you.

You shouldn't hit him like that, Edgar.

You heard his smart mouth. You heard what he called me.

What did you call your father?

Spoor.

Spoor. Where'd you hear a word like that? What kind of word is that?

It's the trail they follow when they hunt some elephant or something.

The pee and poop, and I better not hear it in your mouth again or next time I'll give you more than a love tap. Now finish your dinner.

Nothing but the sound of chewing, of forks cutting meatloaf, the quietest dinnertime in America that evening, none of us kids even breathing till we heard the signal to leave the table. My visceral anger, my sense of being publicly humiliated, the sting of the blow reminding me to "honor thy father" were easily forgiven, if not so easily forgotten. My father seldom hit me once I'd outgrown short pants, and I wasn't stupid enough to challenge him once I'd started wearing long pants, so the few times I did get popped are checkpoints that help me reconstruct the hazy outline of adolescence.

Less easy to forgive is what my father did with my word gleaned from the Tarzan books. How he changed its meaning, used it against me. I hadn't intended to call him a piece of shit or a piss puddle. Hadn't even considered *spoor* as a thing. Spoor to me meant something vaporous, like a cooking odor or the cloud a woman wearing too much perfume leaves behind in a room. Airy like that. An unpleasant smell, armpit, toejam, funky, yes, but nothing as concrete as an actual turd in the bushes you could step on, smear all over your jungle boots. Calling my father a stinky smell was about equal plus a little bit extra to him calling me a knucklehead or whatever comic-strip word he'd used to characterize the dumb thing I'd done in my mother's tale. His translation of *spoor* removed play from the word, put it in a context I hadn't intended, put other words in my mouth, nasty words he felt obligated to punish me for saying and dare me to repeat. What bothered me not a little was the suspicion he might be correct. The incident might have revealed he knew something about spoor I didn't. And what you didn't know, could hurt you. And what you thought you did know, could hurt you too. The trickiness of words, the ownership of words was tied up with this confusion and menace. Part and parcel, root and branch.

Whether or not such a textbook-clear lesson registered for me that night at the dinner table is questionable. Stories are onions. You peel one skin and another grins up at you. And peeling onions can make grown men cry. Which raises other questions. Why does one transparent skin on top of another transparent skin, layer after layer you can see through if each is held up to the light, why are they opaque when bound one on top of the other to form an onion or story? Like a sentence with seven clear, simple words and you understand each word but the meaning of the sentence totally eludes you. You might suggest there is no light source at the core of the onion, nothing similar to a lamp that can be switched on so you can see from outside in. Or you might say an onion is the light and the truth, or at least as much truth and light as you're ever going to receive on this earth, source and finished product all rounded into one and that's the beauty of solid objects you can hold in your hand. Peeling away layers turns them into something less, something other, always. Each skin, each layer a different story, connected to the particular, actual onion you once held whole in your hand as the onion is connected to stars, dinosaurs, bicycles, a loon's cry, to the seed it sprouted from, the earth where the seed rotted and died and slept until it began dreaming of being an onion again, dreamed the steps it would have to climb, the skins it would have to shed and grow to let its light shine again in the world.

AT THE BEGINNING OF *THINGS FALL APART* CHINUA Achebe mentions a story the people of Umofia pass down from generation to generation, concerning the founder of their clan, the ancestor who wrestled a spirit of the wild for seven days and seven nights, earning for himself and his descendants the right to settle on the land they've occupied ever since. Told countless times, countless ways, in each recounting the fabled bout happens again, not in the past, but alive and present in Great Time, the always present tense of narrative where every alternative is possible, where the quick and the dead meet, where all stories are true. The wrestling match between Okonkwo and Amalinze described in the first paragraph of Achebe's novel is an intersection like the one drawn with chalk on an earthen floor to summon Loa, like the crossroads sacred to Damballah where living and dead pass one another, like the X Malcolm chose to signify being lost and found, a symbol of transfiguration, one identity dying into new hope, new life, a new name yet to be spoken.

The story of Okonkwo throwing Amalinze recalls the story of the Founder defeating the spirit of the wild. Present substantiates past, past verifies the present. In the rhythms of Achebe's prose, in African drums or prayers or chants or oratory, confirmation is received through the senses that the ancestral spirits live, the wrestlers sweat again, flesh smacks flesh, watchers cheer, gathered in a circle around the threshing ground where bodies are flung and fling themselves into patterns as familiar and unpredictable as the steps of jazz dance, the choreography of a fast-break slam dunk on a playground basketball court. This happened once in a certain righteous fashion and thus produces what you see here, striving to happen righteously again. Father son. Son father.

No wrestler truly shines unless he wears the Founder's glistening skin. The Founder's body lies inert, forgotten until the teller of the tale animates the legend with bodies of strong, young men crouched in the ancient postures of hand-to-hand combat.

Father stories are about establishing origins and through them legitimizing claims of ownership, of occupancy and identity. They connect what's momentary and passing to what surpasses, materiality to ideal. Achebe teaches how simple and profoundly necessary such stories are. Men's stories, women's stories. How they are about blood and roots and earth, how they must be repeated each generation or they are lost forever. If the stories dim or disappear altogether, a people's greatness diminishes, each of us becomes a solitary actor. The fighter fights alone, for riches or survival, or finds himself a puffed-up brawler, a sideshow performer of other people's stories about themselves, if there is no chorus remembering, connecting him to Great Time.

Who are the truly dead? Chinua Achebe is the African voice, the conduit of traditional wisdom that teaches the dead are those who don't speak and are not spoken of, those not connected by vital words, those whom the stories have forgotten, who have forgotten the stories. Why am I in this American land? Why do I claim it? Why should anyone respect my claim, respect me? Who listens when I speak? Who will treat my story not as entertainment, not as a product to be sold or consumed? Who is listening and searching as I am for a father's voice, not to prove anything to anybody, but so it will be remembered. Live on.

Black South Africans call Mandela "the Old Man." One meaning of this affectionate title is quite literal. We've been in this land a long time because here is this old man, our Father, and he had fathers and those fathers had fathers and we go back as far as the stories they have told us, we could tell you. Stories about a greatness which may be obscured temporarily but will shine again because here in the flesh is this young old man who has arrived to remind us who we are. He quickens our deadened spirits with force far older than his many years. Old Man. Father. A great door to a temple, intricately carved with figures from our history—queens, kings, scenes of triumph, warriors, gods—an ancient door swinging open to let in the new day.

The stories must be told. Ideas of manhood, true and transforming, grow out of private, personal exchanges between fathers and sons. Yet for generations of black men in America this privacy, this privilege has been systematically breached in a most shameful and public way. Not only breached, but brutally usurped, mediated by murder, mayhem, misinformation. Generation after generation of black men, deprived of the voices of their fathers, are for all intents and purposes born semi-orphans. Mama's baby, Daddy's maybe. Fathers in exile, in hiding, on the run, anonymous, undetermined, dead. The lost fathers cannot claim their sons, speak to them about growing up, until the fathers claim their own manhood. Speak first to themselves, then unambiguously to their sons. Arrayed against the possibility of conversation between fathers and sons is the country they inhabit, everywhere proclaiming the inadequacy of black fathers, their lack of manhood in almost every sense the term's understood here in America. The power to speak, father to son, is mediated or withheld; white men, and the reality they subscribe to, stand in the way. Whites own the country, run the country, and in this world where possessions count more than people, where law values property more than person, the material reality speaks plainly to anyone who's paying attention, especially black boys who own nothing, whose fathers, relegated to the margins, are empty-handed ghosts.

Rather than experience the shame of encounters whose archetype is the child visiting prison, speaking to his incarcerated father through a baffle in a filthy Plexiglas screen, the man, the boy learn to protect themselves. It's no mystery to me why my father almost never visits his son, my brother, in Western Penitentiary. By engaging in a kind of self-destructive self-policing, fathers and sons enforce, perpetuate the walls between them. Deny each other to deny the lacerating ground upon which they are forced to meet: the prison imprinted in their collective past, looming in their future. Of course, denial doesn't remove the problem. As long as injustice persists and with it the gross disparities between black communities and white communities on all the scales truly a measure of the right to life, the primal exchange, black father to son, son to father, will be obstructed, poisoned.

Let me say it again, in the simplest terms. This country, as it presently functions, stands between black fathers and sons, impeding communication, frustrating development, killing or destroying the bodies and minds of young men, short-circuiting the natural process of growth, maturity, the cycle of the generations. This country, as it's constituted now, today, its basic institutions and values, or rather the corrupted versions of these institutions and values produced by the paradigm of race, has abandoned its children. Though young black men are a highly vulnerable and visible target, fear, hate, neglect, and hypocrisy characterize society's address to all its children. Frustration, anger, rebellion are youth's response. The relation between chattel slaves and those who claimed to own them offers a precise, instructive parallel for contemporary generational conflict. Black styles of dress, speech, body movement, and insurrection are imitated by white kids for many reasons, but one reason is seldom acknowledged. White kids know in their bones black kids are on the point, catching the hell intended to quash all young people. Unless enough of us transform ourselves, subdue our selfishness and shortsightedness and thereby change the direction the country is going, the prospects for young black men, all young people, won't improve.

Young people understand their peril, are voting with their feet. They're long gone. Live and die elsewhere.

Young black men are treated as a problem. A squeaking wheel that needs to be fixed. They join other "problem" populations (the homeless, AIDS victims, drug addicts, criminals, Iraqis, etc.) to form a highly elastic, suspect category. Solutions evolved to deal with these problem groups have a worrisome similarity, nearly as worrisome as the tendency to lump all members of each group and the disparate groups themselves into one undifferentiated mass of "otherness." Solutions are bureaucratized, emanate from the top down. Problem groups are identified as different, and difference is expressed in dangerous, threatening terms. Negative definitions of problem groups depend on the power of the media to simplify and reduce complex issues, the media's license ("freedom of the press") to foreground or bury stories solely on the basis of its self-interest in monopolizing and profiting from its hold on the public's attention. Though fear of the "other" is as old as myth, xenophobia, insecurity, envy, it possesses new force and immediacy once allied with the power of modern media to overwhelm, to think for us when we're too tired, lazy, busy, scared to think for ourselves. Difference becomes deviance becomes division becomes demonization. A campaign is mounted to deter, punish, exile, or eradicate the problem group. The majority view this style of problem solving as rational and just, a necessary policing and maintenance of normalcy. From the point of view of the problem group the issue is survival.

Emotionally charged metaphors drawn from warfare and sport dramatize public discussion of the "problem." The implicit presence of the paradigm of race flickers just beneath the surface, offering its quasi-religious authority to the notion that problem groups are somehow fundamentally different from the rest of us, sanctioning the most drastic solutions to maintain the world as it should be. With the same blind, relentless logic of the computer whirring through the billion off/on choices of its circuitry, the Western mindset seems disposed to conquer by dividing, apprehending the world in polarized terms of either/or.

PARENTS VISCERALLY BOND WITH LIKENESSES THEY discover or invent in tiny, newborn Mary or Tommy all freshly bathed, powdered, and swaddled in hospital linen. This identification, this celebration of self reproduced, self extended yet also miraculously transcended, may be normal and necessary to get us in the proper spirit for the rigors of child rearing. But in America this positive identification with likeness is also the beginning of trouble because we impose a thing called "race" on the face in the cradle. On the basis of observable, external features—lips, nose, color, hair, and paradoxically, even in the absence of these signs if we know the "race" of the parents—a newborn's destiny is assigned. Assumptions about the infant's character, intelligence, ability to launch a jump shot, manage a baseball team or a corporation are swiftly, unalterably ascribed.

If you're a black man gazing through the nursery window at your newborn son, whatever else you're feeling, love, joy, wonder, gratitude, the tipsiness of the universe whirling around you as you step aside, make room for a new star at the dead center, you cannot entirely escape the chill of the cloud passing momentarily between you and your boy. The cloud of *race*.

No, it doesn't pass. It settles in the tiny mirror of the face you're searching, darkens the skin with a threat of bad weather. Sooner or later, whether you're rich or poor, whether your blackness is wrapped in ivory or ebony, you must address this threat: the legacy of being despised, 'buked and scorned, of inequality and powerlessness. You've passed it on to your son. It may become as hateful and corrosive for him as it's been for his fathers. Wealth, position have no bearing on the deep, general levels of resistance he will encounter, except to add a tinge of irony to success, teach the futility of certain compromises, the bitterness of how close to winning losing can be.

Will you be able to protect him from what's dogged you and yours. Are your face, your skin admissions of defeat. Have you failed to redress crimes committed against you. Where is the clean slate upon which he can write his name. Your name.

Sorry is not enough. Sorry won't do. You acknowledge with a sinking feeling—how far, how long you sink is the worst moment, what can't be written—acknowledge how little things have changed. It could drive you wild, the face, the race in the crib is yours and the shit's about to start all over again. He must go out into the world and fight too many of the same battles you did, perhaps bearing the irony of a white name, a pale face that leads to the same compromising, unanswerable questions the darkest orphan in this society of white over black must confront. Who is your father?

You are your son's biological link to past and future. Are you also his burden. To claim you, say yes to you, must he also accept the stigma of race. Does your dark face doom him to be an outsider, force him to address one way or another the lives his fathers, his brothers and sisters have pursued on the margins of society. Damned if he does, damned if he doesn't. If he denies you, he doesn't need to look any farther than the nose on his face, the skin on the back of his hands, to realize he's denying himself. Saying no to himself. No to the power within himself to achieve what no one can give: freedom and equality.

Are you proof he's less than a man because you're not able to give him what white men give to their sons at birth: full, unquestioned, unconditional citizenship. You can attempt to arm him, to prepare him to face the hard facts, but in the innocence of your first glimpses of him, you cannot pretend the facts don't exist. You can't pretend "race" doesn't exist, and "race" defines you both as something other, something less than a white man. All that mess seemed like old news, nasty, sweepable-under-the-rug news, and you could fight it or forget it or just say fuck it until the moment you peer into the mirror of those still unfocused dark eyes. Are you guilty of an unforgivable miscalculation. Have you passed on to him what your daddy passed on to you. The broken circle—unbroken.

I'm making up this father-son exchange. I have no evidence the nursery scene I'm sketching ever happened. No actual father or son may recognize themselves in what I've written. It's as much about a father and daughter as a father and son. Many would deny the relevance, its applicability to their experience. The words and thoughts I attribute to fathers and sons are not drawn directly from my experience, either. As I wrote I listened as much as composed. Stillness spread within me as I entered a space where boundaries are breached. Inner quiet merges with a larger stillness and voices not mine begin to speak, not to me, but through me. I listen, neither affirm nor deny the authenticity of what I'm hearing. The voices are not mine, the story they're unfolding just might be.

No one's asking for sympathy. No tears, no hand wringing or prayers or handouts. I'm setting down part of a story, a small piece of what needs to be remembered so when we make up the next part, imagine our lives, our history, this piece will be there, among the fragments lost, found, and remembered.

The paradigm of race works to create distance between sons and fathers. One of the worst aspects of this distance is the unwitting complicity of the victims perpetuating it. Because we don't talk or can't talk father to son, son to father, each generation approaches the task of becoming men as if no work has been accomplished before. Treats an unfinished building as if it's a decaying, useless building and feels compelled to tear it down, start over, instead of utilizing solid foundations bought and paid for with the ancestor's blood. Imagine how different we might be if we really listened to our fathers' stories. If we preserved them, learned to make them part of our lives. Wouldn't the stories, if known and performed over generations, be infused with the power of our music. Transforming power, engendering power, get-happy and stay-strong power. Power to link us as our music links, power to plant seeds, nurture them, celebrate their growth.

Our fathers' stories, like their songs, their bodies, can be stolen, silenced, alienated from them, sold, corrupted. We must learn to resist those who would come between us, those who would destroy the messages we must pass on.

The novelist Richard Wright suffered a biological uneasiness as he traveled for the first time through Africa in the 1950s. The inadequacy, the failures of his black fathers, the proof of racial inferiority seemed evident everywhere in the ramshackle cities of the Third World. Trains didn't run on time, faucets didn't function or, when they did, dripped unpotable slime. Africa's rawness and clamor were for Wright a chorus of European colonial administrators in his face, jeering, "I told you so." Wright's deepest insecurities and fears, the legacy of his illiterate, brutalized sharecropper father had pursued him, caught up with him, taunted him with nightmarish intensity, ironically, at the very moment Europeans appeared to be ceding control of Africa to Africans. Instead of coming home to Africa, Wright found himself "going home," his vulnerable roots exposed, like a black woman with pressed hair caught in a sudden downpour.

In his autobiography, *Black Boy*, Wright epitomizes one kind of response to the seemingly unbridgeable distance between sons and fathers: "When I tried to talk to him I realized that, though ties of blood made us kin, though I could see a shadow of my face in his face, though there was an echo of my voice in his voice, we were forever strangers, speaking a different language, living on vastly different planes of reality." Wright orphans himself. Repudiating his father, he comes perilously close to repudiating all people of color. He recalls their "dingy palms," their faces "that hurt me because they had become so thoroughly associated in my feelings with hunger and fear." Exhausted, nearly defeated by the lonely struggle with his demons, Wright despairs, allows his voice to deliver a scathing verdict upon his people and himself: "Negroes had never been allowed to catch the full spirit of Western Civilization . . . they lived somehow in it but not of it. And when I brooded upon the cultural barrenness of black life, I wondered if clean, positive tenderness, love, honor, loyalty, and the capacity to remember was native with man."

If black life is inherently different, at best a forlorn, crippled version of white life, perhaps the only way to survive the withering pressures of the southern black culture that produced his father is to escape, run away. Wright leaves his father behind, a memory frozen in time, mired in the red clay of a Mississippi plantation, a pillar of salt turned towards the past. If *Black Boy* doesn't exactly slay the father, it radically displaces him. The King is dead. Long live the King. The black boy flees to the North, proclaims himself an orphan. As author, he steals the Promethean fire, assumes the role of father, creates a world and its inhabitants.

ANOTHER FORM OF RUNNING AWAY IS SUBSTITUTING A white father for the unreachable or unknowable or unacceptable black one. Integration can be interpreted as a scheme for legitimizing a form of conditional adoption. The black orphan, who's never really allowed to forget he is an orphan, is permitted to apply for conditional membership in the white family. With emphasis on the *conditional* clause. Because the main condition is that all power to determine the kind and quality of inclusion rests in the hands of the adoptive white family. A black boy like Supreme Court Justice Clarence Thomas understands early whom he must honor and please if he expects any of the patrimony to trickle down to him. His grandfather, his father (and by extension, his "race") are useful to Justice Thomas, real to him, only in so far as they are a source of skills and stories that smooth his adoption, endear him to his new family. Part of the bargain, another absolute, nonnegotiable condition, is that the orphan may not tote his kinfolk into the house with him. If they must be seen or heard, it may only be at the back door, hat in hand, tapping softly, continuing to act out roles specified by the paradigm of race.

Those whom Malcolm X dubbed "house niggers" expend considerable energy acting out a genocidal fantasy of integration: if they scrupulously imitate the master's ways, identify completely with the master's interests, including his destructive, demeaning fantasies about them, no one will notice the adopted "child" is not one of the master's literal children. Of course some of these orphans are indeed the master's kids, as Malcolm X points out, damning the white devils, whose blood lightened his complexion.

And that's another method of seeking the black father: killing the oppressive white one. As Malcolm did, as Langston Hughes does in various poems, abjuring, denying, excoriating, dismissing the white men who impregnated, abused, deserted their mothers.

Playing other variations on the father-son theme, James Baldwin in *Notes of a Native Son* felt the necessity to remove himself from Richard Wright's spiritual, literary paternity. Baldwin argued that Wright's fiction contains a fatal flaw: though Wright could father a character such as Bigger Thomas, Bigger doesn't possess the capacity to imagine himself Wright's son. Ellison's invisible man retreats underground; he hibernates, splits open like a seed, births himself.

Black fathers, white fathers, both, neither. Submission, rejection, adoption, upstaging, replacing. Black American men seeking surrogate fathers in other countries, continents: Mao, Marx, Che, Gandhi, Mandela, Shaka, extraterrestrial fathers like W. W. Fard. Outer space, inner space, mothers as fathers.

Finally the glaring exception to the rule, not proving

but potentially terminating the rule: sons bonded to other sons in gang families. Youth gangs in the street, on the corner, that murder their own youth, that don't play, don't waste energy seeking fathers, don't need anyone telling them who they are or what to do because they manufacture and enforce their own rules, step into the vacuum and become their own fathers and mothers, creating a world where childhood his disappeared, where the idea of fathers and sons is anachronistic, redundant. For these sons there is no past nor future, only the sheer exhilaration and terror of *now*, the only time that counts, the only time you're ever alive.

But what about the clothes favored by youth gangs, the oversize, droopy, hanging-off-the-shoulder, off-the-behind styles. Kids in stuff way too big, rushed-out-the-door-in-the-morning, don't-care thrown-on-looking stuff, regressive, infantilizing, even to the sorry extreme of accessories like flop-eared baby caps, pacifiers. Styles antithetical to the city—Timberland boots, Pendleton wool shirts. Isn't one message of these costumes loud and clear: *we're still kids*. Not grown yet, nostalgic, needing the care we never had. Ragamuffin orphans who belong to no one, lost in these swaddling clothes. Help us pull ourselves together. Hike up these baggy drawers. Turn my cap around. But if abandonment, a plea for help are projected in styles of dress, there are also the cold, distant eyes, daring you to touch.

.   .   .

A MOTHERFUCKER, AIN'T IT. THIS DADDY SEARCH. Looking for a father under every brick or rock or coal pile and me signifying such a search is the very brick-and-rock foundation of various political philosophies, survival strategies from integration to separation to burn-baby-burn incineration to self-annihilation and starting all over again. Maybe the search for fathers is finally only a trope, a ropa-dope trope containing enough rope to hang you up terminally, you black bastard.

People are easier to kill if they come from nowhere. If they have no names, no fathers or mothers. When great numbers of people are murdered as they were during the high tide of the European slave trade with Africa or the forcible removal of the indigenous inhabitants of North America and Australia or during the Holocaust or the ethnic cleansing today in Eastern Europe, the anonymity of the victims consigns them to oblivion. Nothing has been lost, no crime committed. Rather, a kind of harsh but impersonal justice has been served, the wheel of his-torical inevitability has rotated, as it must, as it has count-less times before, without malice, according to Darwinian imperatives. The dead, the piles of corpses are nobodies who began nowhere, go nowhere, except back where they belong. Nowhere. No-count. Nothing.

Words like *nigger* and *kaffir* are not only insulting but extremely dangerous in a white person's mouth, often in a black's mouth, because such words perform the same work as the killing. They extinguish connection, possibil-ity. They enforce the reality of a world locked down by the rules of the paradigm of race. If you're not already among the dead, when you're called a nigger, you're being softened up for the kill.

Who wants me dead? Who has expended such enormous energy killing my fathers? I've wanted answers to these questions my entire life, and sought them one way or another, but the questions, let alone answers, were so disturbing, it's taken till now to write them down, say the questions, say answers aloud to myself. Let me be precise. I am a victim. An innocent bystander. The fear and hate directed at me and people like me, mine, who are not and never will be white people, that hate and fear, as old and ugly as Europe's original encounters with Africa, were meant for another target. Not me. Hate and fear so intense, ritualized, obsessional, that their closest analogue is love, they compete with love as the most profound emotion one human being can express towards another, hate and fear that powerful must have their source in the deepest, most private, unsayable conversations a person carries on within herself or himself, about himself or herself.

For my so-called *white* countryman, I am the ground against which their figure rises, the *black* defining, proving, enabling their *white*. Though I didn't choose the role, I became a kind of body double, standing in for them in risky scenes or scenes in which they choose not to expose themselves. I represent certain incriminating truths they would just as soon forget, what they hate and fear about themselves. By embodying the negative element of their

split nature, I free them of responsibility for the incestuous mix of angel and devil, spirit and flesh, light and
darkness. I serve as a reminder of what they seek to
exorcise from their souls. But if exorcism produces a new, sanitized self, it also
produces demons. Demons and purity born at the same
instant, from the same metaphorical womb. Twins conceived, confirmed by the same process. Exorcism cuts
the cord, separates evil from good absolutely and just as
absolutely installs good in the driver's seat. Separation of
white *from* black is preparation for white *over* black.

This exorcism, whites attempting to rid themselves of
an evil twin, did not begin in America. In the medieval
night of its soul, Europe had come face to face with
the beast, the dark double in the mirror, the unnerving
presence always of saint/sinner, good/evil, corruptible
flesh/divine spirit.

The European Renaissance imposed light where darkness squatted. Slum clearance. Urban renewal. Taming
the sacred sphere while expanding the secular, objecti-
fying time and space with clocks and linear perspective,
the invention and celebration of Greco-Roman antiquity
as Europe's shining parent, the systematic purging of alternative, pagan realities were attempts to restore harmony to man's soul, dethrone the beast, wipe it from the
mirror.

If the beast proved undeniable, still, it might be possible to cage it. Renaissance culture, its bloom and flow-
ering in the arts, its codification of manners, civility, law,

its moral and ethical speculation, its technological advances, its bureaucratization of trade and commerce established various measuring rods with which man could gauge as well as substantiate his emancipation from the beast, his gradual progress towards imitation of divinity.

The African, once "discovered," was abruptly situated during the Renaissance in an evolving paradigm of race: first as *different*, then *other*, then *inferior*. Caliban and his kin one more measuring rod. With the added advantage of being beasts of burden, not only to perform the heavy-duty work of empire building in New World colonies, but also to bear the psychic weight of guilt and punishment for man's dualism, his warring impulses. Like the regions being zoned at this moment to receive deadly nuclear waste, couldn't these others, these savages, these outsiders absorb the poisonous by-products of the European diaspora. Africans became a perfect foil, a means of systematically distancing, externalizing truths about itself Europe couldn't abide within its soul. Black skin the rag with which Europe cleansed its hands. If Africa had not existed, Europe would have invented her. And did.

I'm a victim, a person on the way to buy a quart of orange juice who happens to walk past a crack house and gets wounded in a drive-by shooting. An outsider, voiceless, unconnected with the feud causing the shooting. Someone external to the action, suddenly seized by it, changed, defined, inextricably linked at the instant shots ring out.

But more victimized even than that because a passerby's jeopardy is bad luck, a case of being in the wrong place at the wrong time, the injuries suffered, to some extent, accidental. Suppose, instead, one of the parties involved in a deadly quarrel over turf or drugs or double cross or sex or honor or whatever, knows his enemy drives by firing every day at precisely 2:27 P.M. Rather than risk a counterattack on his antagonist's lair or move himself to another location or attempt to resolve the dispute, the assaulted party decides to protect himself by forcing his neighbors to form a human wall every day from 2:00 to 3:00. Imagine the quarreling parties are blood relatives, brothers, sisters, imagine a single conflicted person who wants to live and wants to die, to thrive as a drug lord and also extricate himself from the dirty business, a tormented being, a Jekyll and Hyde who is a constant danger to himself and others precisely because he is both, what he thinks he is and also what he pretends he is not. So he figures out a way to defend himself against himself without eradicating his brother, his twin, himself. Imagine how he might explain his strategy to himself, rationalize, justify the bloody heap of bodies on his doorstep, dead people who just yesterday were his neighbors.

The paradigm of race allows basic truths about the social and political nature of America to remain hidden from view, truths about human nature, our capacity for denial, contradiction, selfishness. The habit of division and compartmentalization, separating human beings into those who count and don't count, opens the door to our seemingly bottomless propensity to rationalize self-interest far past the point of absurdity and beyond to self-destruction.

LET'S FACE IT. IT'S IN OUR FACES ALREADY, ANYWAY. Whose child are you? What's your name? American history can be read as a long paternity suit, or series of suits. If the suit fits . . .

Succeeding waves of immigrants each laid claim to the patriarchy, a share of the patrimony. Think of our country as a vast orphanage. The official policy of the institution is to keep its inmates confused by concealing from them their biological origins. Divide and conquer. Spread a lot of ugly rumors about some people's tainted births, glorify other people's impeccable bloodlines. Float some preposterous lies, dress up myth and legend as fact to explain and prove how different some kinds of people are from other kinds. Keep everybody guessing, confused, under suspicion.

Then devise the paradigm of race. For the majority of Americans the issues of paternity and patrimony are settled. To be white is to be connected to the Great White Father, the ultimate source of power, privilege, and legitimacy. For the minority who can't claim to be white, the issue is also settled. But less happily.

In America people of color walk under a cloud of unsettled paternity. Assertions that the devil or orangutans engendered us are not heard often today, yet the cloud still accompanies us wherever we go, like an invisible balloon on an invisible string. Even when no one mentions the cloud or pretends it's not there or declares they don't notice or care, everybody's aware of the cloud. Its presence is attested to by our obsession with color. We're color-struck. Stricken by color. More terms for our color than Eskimo languages have invented for snow. *Shit-skin* is one particularly evocative appellation I came across recently in the novel *Clockers* by Richard Price.

Color's been here far longer than the notion of race, and color in itself is of course nothing to be ashamed of. However, the paradigm of race transforms color into a sign of class, culture, and inferiority. Minor skirmishes over naming our color—black, Negro, African American, colored—are meaningless unless we remove the cloud. The cloud has a mighty, damning stretch. Obscures us all. Somewhere, lost in that cloud or separated from us by its darkness, our fathers reside.

BY AND BY WE'LL UNDERSTAND IT BETTER. BY AND BY. Maybe. What I understand now is each and every one of the ways we contrive to compensate for the lost father has its benefits and also potential to consign us to hell. None will do, finally. None can replace the story, the understanding, the words fathers and sons must exchange directly. Face to face. By and by.

FARTHER ALONG WE'LL KNOW MORE ABOUT YOU. . . . TILL I was grown I heard "Fatheralong" and thought Fatheralong was God's name in this hymn, the mysterious God who dwelled in Homewood A. M. E. Z. church, a God I'd meet up with some day and He'd understand and say Well done. Also, I thought of my father, Edgar Wideman, his doubleness, his two-personedness, a man who lived in our house, who in a way ruled it, yet also lived somewhere else, distant, unknown. Another person altogether, *Fatheralong*, I could fathom only indirectly through what he did and said in our house. A stranger's aura about him even when I was close enough to touch him. A familiar stranger. Unpredictable, vaguely threatening, not only because of his size (big) or manner (hard) or color (dark brown contrasting with my mother's paleness) but because my relationship with him differed emphatically from my relationship to my mother.

She was always there. With me. If she had disappeared, no *there* would exist. My world began and ended with her presence. She tucked me in at night, mornings wouldn't commence till my daydreaming, half-sleep haze was punctuated by her feet hitting the floor, her sizzling pee, the toilet flushed, rattle of pots and pans, water running for coffee. If we were separated for some reason, five minutes, a whole afternoon, a rare night I spent in somebody else's house, visualizing myself as my mother might see me was the surest way to make myself feel real. I never talked a lot about my feelings to anyone, but inside my head I maintained a running dialogue with my mother.

When I found myself in novel situations, I often tried to translate what I was experiencing into a story I might tell her. Whether or not I actually narrated the tale to her or anyone else, I wound up explaining things to myself by explaining them to her. She was *there*, like the internal words and rhythm of consciousness are there. A closeness and intimacy the opposite of oppressive, since her presence freed me, helped me grow and expand.

My father, present or not, evoked boundaries. The rules of the house. My duties, chores, responsibilities. The man I must become some day. He was part enforcer, part the physical embodiment of bad news: the world and people in it don't always love you. And further, those people out there counted. They were people who wouldn't hesitate to make themselves heard and felt. In a way he was one of them, carried their weight, brought it inside our house. He left our house to join them, knew the secrets of moving in their world, maybe even preferred it to ours, since he spent plenty of time out there with them. Aspects of him remained enigmatic precisely because they anchored him to unknown places. He didn't invite me to share whatever he'd found, didn't seem to care whether I desired a portion or not. I was certain my mother needed me. My father never expressed such a need. He got along quite nicely, thank you, for hours, days, without me. If he loved me, it definitely wasn't mother love, the love of my aunts and grandmothers. He was definitely somebody else. His love a different love, *Fatheralong*, and what exactly that meant I didn't understand. Tried not to worry it too much. Yet it vexed me, kept me guessing, on my toes. Still, "Farther Along" was one of my favorite gospel songs then and now. I'd be a millionaire today if I could have collected a dime each time I've heard the opening of Sam Cooke's version. His tenor arching like a rainbow over the march-time stride of "Farther Along."

Substituting *father* for *farther*, perhaps I blundered into the song's meaning in spite of myself. After all, isn't it about resignation, learning to wait and trust and endure? To love the imminent revelation, that great getting-up morning surely, surely coming, even though just as surely you won't know it till it hits you. By and by is when it arrives, by and by, the unbound Great Time of our African ancestors.

Is suffering, bearing up under burdens, the only way to learn (earn) the Father's name, his dispensation? No path except a long arc of patience and suffering the Father resolves in his own good, by-and-by time. On time. A snap and promise and sweetness in the music. My father's voice calling, "Get on board." Foretaste of peace and understanding. What I heard Bob Marley singing years later: *One bright morning when my work is over/I will fly away home.*

L i t t l e m a n

MY GREAT-GRANDFATHER DIED WITH HIS MOUTH WIDE
open. They had to tie a string around his jaw to keep it
shut for the wake and funeral. Littleman, who is also
James Harris and also a first cousin to my father, a fact I
didn't figure out for fifty years, remembers the day my
great-grandfather died. We are sitting in a room in the
Greenwood, South Carolina, Holiday Inn, James and myself on matching oatmeal-colored chairs flanking a table
under the room's one window, my father on the edge of
one of the twin doubles with bedspreads that match the
curtains, that match the chairs. Littleman was only five
or six when the old man died, he tells us. Lived with his
mother, my grandfather's sister, just down the road a
piece from the Reverend T. W. Wideman. The Reverend

Tatum W. Wideman and his wife had raised six children in their big house, including my grandfather, Hannibal (Harry), and his sister, Matty, the mother of James. Two of my grandfather's brothers, their wives, and kids boarded with the Reverend, and James was playing in the yard with his cousins when he heard commotion in the house. A shriek. Then shouts and loud crying.

Nobody noticed James as he tipped inside and halted at the threshold of the big front room where the old man's bed was situated to command a view of all comings and goings. Grown-ups were wringing their hands, hugging and holding on to one another. Nobody seemed able to stand still. Bodies stumbling, darting off every which way while James stared at the stillness of his grandfather openmouthed on the bed. Bodies swaying and bumping and entwined, a turmoil of thick shoulders and heavy hips, but when the sea parted James got a good enough look to study the dead man's face, to bring it sixty years forward in time with his testimony in the motel room. He watched them force the jaws shut. Tie a string around his grandfather's head.

More, much more happened that day, but James reminds us he was nothing but a boy. Wasn't sure now, after all these years, if it had been the undertaker who tied the string or somebody from the house or both, the light, bright, almost white undertaker experienced in these matters undoing the first string, tying his better, surer knot. And his not with just any old piece of string, but clean white cord from a kitchen drawer a dignified man like the Reverend Tatum W. Wideman who wore a suit Saturday and Sunday and drove his own one-horse buggy could deal with, if there had to be a cord.

I'm speculating, wondering, imagining as Littleman speaks. But part of me still as my great-grandfather on the four-poster bed, still and gaping. What else? What else? A silent scream. The great rush of emptiness in, then out. What else? Silence always the final word as the jaws work to do the last two things. Expel what's left of life. Receive the abyss. Expel the last unspoken word they ache to form, the breath speeding away you cannot believe is the last one so you chase after it like a shop-keeper who's being robbed. *Stop. Stop, thief.* It's been so long, always, the quickness of the end stuns you, you're open-mouthed with surprise. The great push outward freeing you of all your troubles, the body's impatient weight hurtling through a needle's eye. *Expelling* one of the two last things, and its mirror twin, the inrush, as you wince, are cracked wide open, *receiving* the abyss, the vast knowledge your body needs to remember in order to unbind, unleash itself, return power to its billion, billion separate wills, the single-minded universes your blood and spirit and heart yoke together till the clock strikes, the party's over.

Littleman talks slowly, pauses between words that sometimes take the form of extensions almost sung at the ends of phrases and words, or half-moaned, softly chanted intros to the word about to be spoken. Pauses so he can search, savor what's happening as he listens with you to what he's able to say, what he can't say. What's spoken always a compound of both said and unsaid, silence a sweet marrow within the bones or flesh on the bones of his words. Littleman's story there in the Holiday Inn for all three of us to hear, but only in the separate words each says to himself, words you could think of as marking the distance each of us from the other, each in a different locked room, but also binding us as oddly, inconclusively, compellingly as the blood ties and names we've sat down together in this motel room in South Carolina to summon.

Measured a better word than *slow* to describe the cadence of Littleman's speech. The same relaxed rhythm an appreciative whiskey drinker employs consuming Chivas Regal. That undersea, unhurried poise of swimmers and scuba divers whose limbs have adjusted to the gravity of an element denser than air. A southern way, an African, South Carolinian way of lengthening vowels into diphthongs (two sounds), transforming, elaborating syllables that are simpler, faster in dialects regarded as standard. Rather than fight the density, he swims with the current of words. Listens to himself, not out of self-consciousness but because the language can feel kind of good rolling off your tongue if you let it, ease up and let it carry you, you and not you, recalling your story told by yourself or heard before in another person's telling, a back porch or parlor resurrected as you remember how your story began once, consider where it might go this time. You take your time, give memories an opportunity to sashay in and out, echo and instruct or fuss with other words, other versions. You relax into the thickness that holds all the stories, holds you and works with you if you work with it, slowly, on time. Grunt and shake your head, *no, not that now, not yet,* and look off at a place no one else can see and laugh and use your hands a lot. Laugh at yourself. *Look in there and ax myself what a white man doing upside my granddaddy's bed. Scared me. What a white man ghost doing in the house.* Twirl the ice in your glass with your finger and take a sip. Story won't go nowhere till you get back to it. Story ain't going nowhere without you.

We'd located Littleman by going to church. Life in Promised Land, since the community's founding early in the 1870s, had always revolved around its churches. First a brush arbor, then a succession of solid, tidy buildings, Mount Zion A.M.E. had stood since 1875 on an acre of land sold to the Mount Zion trustees by James Field, one of the first freedmen to buy a section of the Marshall tract. By 1873, forty-four of fifty farms on acreage once comprising the Marshall Plantation had been purchased by freedmen and their families from the South Carolina Land Commission, a creation of the post–Civil War Republican legislature, itself a product of federally supervised elections in which large numbers of former slaves voted for the first time. The walk from any of these farms to Mount Zion was no more than two miles.

For a moment in time, Promised Land, as its name proclaimed, embodied the Reconstruction ideal of land redistribution and black autonomy. Throughout the former Confederacy the phrase "forty acres and a mule" had come to symbolize the dream of reparations for past exploitation and suffering, a foundation for an uncertain future. The freedmen's precarious existence in a hostile, defeated South would be stabilized by land ownership. The land commission, authorized by the South Carolina legislature, would buy land for resale to freedmen. With less than ten percent of the land in the Piedmont region available for sale through this plan, the Marshall tracts offered an unusual opportunity and the response was enthusiastic. Profiteering, swindles, rip-offs tainted the "Promise" from the beginning. In spite of inflated appraisals of poor land, interest-heavy payments exacted from freedmen, the dishonesty of public officials, violence and intimidation by white vigilantes, lack of financial resources, freedmen signed promissory notes to purchase land, built a community of small farms, established churches and schools. Promised Land grew rapidly to eighty-nine households by 1880.

From the church records of Mount Zion—annual conference reports, treasurers' ledgers, baptisms, funerals, weddings, etc., etc.—one history of the Promised Land community could be gleaned. In the voices, songs, and stories of the present generation of churchgoers, another kind of documentation reifies the past. My father and I had hoped we'd get a jump on our researches into family history by attending services at Mount Zion, introducing ourselves to the pastor, explaining our mission, and asking him to announce it to the congregation so we could meet with church members willing and able to assist us.

Our first full day in Promised Land was a Sunday, bright and clear and crisp, unseasonably cool for mid-October. We'd packed church clothes and wore them as we exited the Greenwood Holiday Inn, our base during the stay in South Carolina. Driving towards the center of town, we searched for the elusive turnoff that would take us back to Promised Land. Staff at the motel knew the location of Promised Land and attempted to be helpful, offered us lengthy, detailed directions. Trouble was, nobody's directions exactly matched anybody else's. Right or left out of the Holiday Inn. Turn after the big green bank sign in the center of town. Turn after you get all the way through town. Just stay on the main drag runs along the motel you'll see a sign for the bypass and next street's where you pick up 10. Only tricky part's once you go left there's a school, then a firehouse. Wind on past the BP station, the car wash, and you'll come up on the intersection of Route 10 and then it's a straight shot.

During our five days of shuttling from Greenwood to Abbeville to Promised Land to Greenwood to Abbeville and numerous points beyond and between, we'd discover everybody's directions were correct. Straight shot or bypass or backroads or dogleg of two intersecting highways, all roads didn't exactly lead to Promised Land, but we got lost numerous times and eventually we'd reach some juncture one of us would believe he recognized from somebody's directions and its vague familiarity would encourage us to persevere, think we might even be on track, help us recall a former decision, right or left we'd made at this point, right or wrong, and we'd repeat it or its opposite if we suspicioned we'd made a mistake before. The patchwork of everybody's generous advice like too many layers of clothes on a day starting cool that turns hot; we'd sweat awhile and peel and shuck, arrive at our destination anyway, in spite of, with the aid of, thank you.

After two or three excursions to Promised Land, each by a different route, I realized a simple fact: no road sign in Greenwood pointed the way to Promised Land. People black and white busied around quite aware of Promised Land, the presence and proximity of a satellite black community off Route 10, straddling the railroad tracks, yet there existed no official highway department sign to guide you, indicate you could get there from here. On Route 10 twelve miles beyond Greenwood in a south-westerly direction, if you were looking for it and paying close attention, a Promised Land sign would pop up on your left, indicating a fork in the road you've probably already missed once you've read the Promised Land marker. Zora Neale Hurston's version of the folk maxim "You got to go there to know there" might draw as accurate a map as any proffered by our kind Greenwood hosts.

You won't find Promised Land on most maps, just as you won't discover any mention of Africans or slaves or slavery in the closely printed eight-page outline of the "Chronological History of South Carolina (1662–1825)" that serves as a standard research guide in the Greenwood public library.

Perhaps that's okay, perhaps it's better Promised Land does not appear on most maps. Maybe Promised Land lies where it does to teach us the inadequacy of maps we don't make ourselves, teach us the necessity of new maps, teach us how to create them, reimagine connections others have forgotten or hidden. Maybe we need Promised Land to be born again, 120 years after its founding, the only word on a blank page, a word not written yet, not completely spelled out, one around which, upon which rock we'll begin to inscribe a new story. Is the absence of signs to Promised Land a sin of omission or commission. Or perhaps living next to Promised Land for over a century and not officially acknowledging its location is also denying what it means, how its life touches the lives of those who pretend no path takes you from here to there, those who have constructed a landscape for themselves bereft of signs, who give knowledgeable, neighborly directions to strangers, yet censor from themselves this information they dispense. Is Promised Land, itself, a sign of denial, of terrible misgivings, of a past and present unhinged.

Perhaps Promised Land is one of the maps I've returned to South Carolina with my father to learn to read. Or draw, even as we search.

Littleman wasn't a member of Mount Zion, but there we received confirmation he was alive and well, a member of Lil Zion, just down the road. Probably on his way after services at that off-shoot of Mount Zion, to his lady's house. Littleman beat us to Miss Gladys's place by only a couple minutes. None of us could stop grinning, including Miss Gladys, Littleman's lady, and we made a date to meet the next day in Greenwood at our motel, three of us for sure, four if Miss Gladys could get off from work and join us later.

On Saturday, the day we'd flown from Pittsburgh to
Charlotte, North Carolina, rented a car, and cut down
through South Carolina to Promised Land, my father had
remembered Littleman. We'd detoured through Abbeville, the county seat, checked out its courthouse, finally
arriving around 3:00 at the Crossroads general store in
Promised Land. From old folks at the store we'd received
leads we followed, in a hit-or-miss, spur-of-the-moment
cruise, sight-seeing, gradually acclimating ourselves to
the area surrounding Promised Land, suburbanlike houses
with expansive green lawns, giving way over the course
of a few miles to sparsely settled rural areas, small farms,
long stretches of monotonous new-growth pine woods,
stubbled fields, occasionally the surprise of a huge ante-
bellum mansion with its avenue of magnolia trees domi-
nating a crossroads, one-room shacks that might have
been slave cabins, small homesteads festooned with
makeshift additions, circled by sprawls of old vehicles
and parts of vehicles, piles and mounds of stuff an arche-
ologist could pick through and reconstruct desperate,
miniature epics of ingenuity, dogged, make-do survival.

My father had remembered Littleman during our no-
agenda wandering that first afternoon, in the course of a
conversation he was having with a man I'd given up on.
An old man, hospitable like everyone we'd encountered
that first meandering day in and around Promised Land,
he'd set us down in his living room on a sofa I was
sure had been salvaged from a junked car. He wasn't a
Wideman, but at the former Promised Land schoolhouse

that had been converted to a community center when local schools were integrated, we learned from alumni who were gathering there from across the country for the big annual reunion that most all the Widemans been gone from Promised Land a good long while and Mr. Brown one of the few old-timers, still alive and talking, who might have memories of my grandfather's people.

Mr. Brown nodded a lot, endlessly repeated variations on two or three all-purpose exclamations I hadn't deciphered after fifteen minutes in his home. My father had taken over, decided to explain minutely in far greater detail than I'd known he had worked out, our reasons for traveling to South Carolina, our plan for investigating our family's history. Then he launched into a summary of the events and meaning of that history I'd never heard from him before. The more Mr. Brown nodded, the more inspired my dad became. He was making up the story as he went along, embellishing fragments I'd learned and shared with him, drawing from his own reading, from TV and movies and barbershop, hanging-on-the-corner communal lore and anecdote, a metahistory of the South, slavery, the Wideman clan's heroic resistance to oppression, a tradition of family solidarity my father claimed as his inheritance and vowed to pass on.

I was annoyed on two counts: my father's impassioned summary had minimal basis in the facts as I knew them, and even if it did, he was wasting precious time squandering his account on a nice old gentleman whose capacity to comprehend even a smidgeon of the elaborate tale was suspect. Stop the bullshit and let's get out of here, a mantra ringing inside my head as regularly as the old man's nods and grunts. So I missed what connected my father and Mr. Brown.

We stood outside the man's trailerlike shack, its inside walls unfinished, tar paper dangling in strips from bare boards, in a yard full of odds and ends that must have been collecting for decades, my father still spinning a stirring saga, Mr. Brown either entranced or half-asleep on his feet, mostly the latter, it seemed to me out of the corner of the one eye I'd allotted for keeping track of my elders. I steadily edged towards the rental car, scraping my feet in a patch of gravel, coughing, hrumping, hoping my father was ready at last to disengage and follow. This kind of monologuing and monopolizing wouldn't do. If this relic of Mr. Brown could have told us anything, if he ever had anything to reveal, we'd botched the chance to draw him out. My father's rap had smothered the poor old guy. I'd have to figure a way to let my father know our time in Promised Land was short and we couldn't afford to waste it. Without being bossy or disrespectful I needed to get his attention, convince him to stay on track, follow my lead when we questioned informants.

Then I noticed the conversation had changed. They were talking to each other about Littleman, an animated exchange about an actual person they both knew and I knew, too. My father hadn't mentioned Littleman in connection with our trip. I'd never made the association, either. The two men nodding and smiling and shaking hands behind me had conjured Littleman out of thin air. In their own way. And I'd missed it completely. In their own way, a way excluding me, chastising me because I'd been so busy dismissing it out of hand.

Oh yeah. Yes indeed. He's my cousin. Yeah. They call him Littleman, just like you said. Littleman. James Harris. Worked with my daddy. Uh-huh. Sure. He was from down here. Short, brown-skinned man. Good ole James. You know who I'm talking about. Sure you do.

Mr. Brown couldn't say where Littleman stayed, but he's sure nuff round here. Yes indeed. Yup. Yup. James Harris. Nodding when he croaked the name like James Harris a tall stake he's driving in the ground with his blue-black forehead.

BOY, OH BOY. I'M GLAD I REMEMBERED OLD JAMES. DON'T know why I didn't think of him before. Lives close around here somewhere. Mr. Brown sees him. You remember James. Sam and Warren and James all worked for Grandpa when you were little. And when you weren't so little. Everybody called him "Littleman." Your grandfather brought him and two other fellows up to Pittsburgh one summer after he'd been down here to visit. The others left but James stayed three or four years . . . maybe more. Probably been down here since. Twenty-five, thirty years. He could tell us all about the family. Raised here. Can't think to save my life of the name of the bar on Wylie Avenue where Warren hung out. I'd run into

Littleman in there sometimes. Why didn't I think of him before. Bet he'll be a big help. Uh-huh. He drove Grandpa's truck. I know you know him.

I couldn't recall if I'd ever known his name was James Harris, it sounded familiar, but no doubt about the time, my lonely first semester at the University of Pennsylvania, Littleman had driven my mother, grandfather, and high-school sweetheart Jeanne to Philadelphia for homecoming weekend. That crazy, long-lost weekend Jeanne and I had spent, mostly unsuccessfully, trying to sneak away from everybody else, hit me first, then lots else I knew about Littleman flashing in neon fits and starts. Yes. He'd come up fresh from South Carolina. Yes. I was his helper on Grandpa's truck. He'd honk once every weekday morning, early, just me and my mother in the kitchen, the red pickup at the curb. His funny country accent. His habit of calling me by all my entitles, *John Edgar*, embarrassing me if anybody else was around to hear him say my name the old-fashioned, down-home way my grandfather said it. A ladder of skewered kielbasy grilling in the window of a hole-in-the-wall bar on the North Side of Pittsburgh where we ate lunch. He'd never called my grandfather "Uncle Harry" then, at least not in my hearing. Always said "Mr. Wideman." Somehow I guess I must have known we were related . . . distantly, obscurely, I would have assumed, not at all anxious to tie myself too closely in any way, shape, or fashion to the old country of the South. Littleman. Of course I remembered. How had I ever forgotten.

A few quick, defining strokes and the memory sketch

of Littleman turned three-dimensional, a walking, talking person. As magical as the sudden resurrection of this man I'd known quite well once, but had forgotten almost totally, was the equally sudden and unforeseen presence of a person I realized I really knew nothing about. My ignorance, everything I didn't know about Littleman, what I'd never asked nor considered confronted me just as insistently as the flood of recollections.

RETURNING TO THE SOUTH I AM TRYING TO ENCOUN-ter what part the region plays in the economy of my being. The South is a parent, an engenderer, part of the mind I think with, the mind thinking me. My history begins here, at least my history in this hemisphere, on this continent, this New World. Here I experienced the pangs of separation from one culture, the shock of or-phanhood, the grudging adoption, inculcation, force-feeding of another culture. I suffered imprinting of a social matrix, absorbed models of feeling, deportment, speech. Here is the place where I learned the necessity of setting out again to find a new home in a vast migration outward, away, that could also be understood later as a means of finding a path inward, back to origins, a terri-tory in my mind I could call home.

History is not something given, a fixed, chronological, linear outline with blank spots waiting to be filled with newly unearthed facts. It's the activity over time of all the minds comprising it, the sum of these parts that pro-duces a greater ecological whole. History, the past, is what you're thinking, what you've thought. *You,* the individual, you the enabler and product of the collective enterprise of mind.

History is mind, is driven by mind in the same sense a flock of migratory birds, its configuration, destination, purpose, destiny are propelled, guided by the collective mind of members of the immediate flock and also the species, all kindred birds past and present inhabiting Great Time. Collective experience feeds this "mind" with a sort of accumulated, biological, experiential wisdom, knowledge both within and external to individuals. The minute-by-minute precarious survival of each individual is also work that insures perpetuation of kind. Conscious articulation of common goals, common stakes in a common struggle to survive is one means of acknowledging and also building upon the past, asserting a sense of belongingness to something greater than ourselves.

Just as swallows eventually figured out how to fly to Capistrano, the historical mind of African people captive in the American South learned how to "get over." From daily encounters with this land, its peoples, weather, its tasks, this "mind" fashioned visions, dreams, an immaterial, spiritual realm with the density, the hard and fast integrity of rungs on an iron ladder. Invisible ladders leaning on air with iron rungs people could climb. The unwillingness of southern whites to share or cede space or acknowledge black humanity, their unrestrained power to do harm, to murder, steal, rape, these were palpable barriers embodied in the southern landscape, real as distance, swamps, forests, rivers, night. The minds of my forebears found means to negotiate paths over, under, around, and through this resistance, this danger, envisioned "freedom," the possibility of transcending all barriers, even as they were being conditioned to believe the barriers weren't there or should be there, even when the punishment for conceiving the barriers, let alone naming or resisting them, was death.

The South Carolina outside the rental-car window, the pine forests, meadows, and pastures, the soft rolling contours of lushly arable fields, this land cultivated and divided, consecrated to the well-being of its owners, projects ideas of property, prosperity, of substance and continuity of family, security, wealth. This message spoken by the land today is one voice among many, one conception of past and present my father and I hear as we drive. Within that voice-over, older, fainter, yet undeniably audible if you teach yourself to listen, to speak its language, another presence is enfolded. This older presence of cruelty, doubt, and conflict dyes the land different colors than those the bright October light reveals.

Certitude like a swift, chilly draft from an unknown source prickles my skin. I've been here before. I'm not simply summoning up some reactionary, old-time, morbid stereotype of slavery days to mock the New South. I've been here before. My skin recalls sensations I can't name yet.

When I was here before I pressed my body into every conceivable nook and cranny, dove in the creeks, climbed trees. I stood naked and bleeding beside a stump, a sack strap rubbed a hole in my shoulder, my fingers dug cold meat from somebody's half-eaten, half-chewed, discarded dinner. I wept good-bye to loved ones crowded onto a steamboat headed to hell. Tore the raggedy tail from my only shirt and watched the grimy flag flutter down to the mound of earth under which my woman lay, praying she'd carry my offering back across the great waters to the old ones, praying they'd call soon for me. These images borne, remembered in this land that was also a blank tablet, a new beginning, in spite of pain flickering always like a light source trained on the screen where I watch my life.

Think of a warm summer night, the darkness blinking its thousand eyes at you, as within a wooded field heaven's vault has plunged and hovers six feet off the ground. Fireflies are stars struck like matches against the blackness, dying and being born, our many lives here, some spared, some brutally, randomly extinguished as we decided what to make of this place where we found ourselves, the bondage, the abuse, the buying and selling of our bodies, as long as we could think past it, think other and beyond it, did not stop our transformation of the land, curb our power to transform ourselves.

We altered rivers, filled in valleys, drained swamps, cleared forests, dug canals, cut roads. The evidence of us moving doggedly, enormously as termite armies, transforming the physical shape of this land is everywhere. No mean feat but it pales, or rather it's only the tip of the iceberg when you look closer, think more deeply, peer into the nonmaterial medium supporting the physical aspects of this world, what reaches under our feet, sustains us as we imagine walking on water.

Our screams and lost children, the carriages we drove, linen we washed, animals we hunted, gutted, and cooked, mansions we planned and built, the lies, forced migrations, fucking, the wars with Indians and philosophical, theological speculations, our diseases, dreams—in short, our condition—filled us, the survivors and ones who didn't survive except in us, through us, filled us with memories and expectations of a land that could be no other than the one we needed, the one we fashioned to survive. The effort of grasping what was here and who was here and what needed to be done if we were to last more than one generation in this wilderness forced us to imagine a world which would sustain us. We forged correspondences between external and internal visions. Contrived a match between what we found and what we found necessary. Mind was the key. Mind can unlock the correspondences now. They are packed beneath the surfaces of other appearances, stories layered within other stories these appearances try to tell us.

Pine trees, sinuous, sparkling creeks, fields abandoned to stubble and snowy cotton flowers. Graveyards buried behind, within other graveyards. All the missing African names of things, the things themselves present, renamed. Our bodies, precious, beautiful because we read our history in them. Not always a pleasant story, but upbeat finally because here we come today, walking, talking, through the town square of Abbeville—big bosoms, round butts, big feet, tribal markings of our inherited features, more lasting, distinctive, and decorative than any knife could carve. We fashioned alternative realities no more supernatural than the rhythm of blood and sinew and muscle of the enraptured, doomed body inside the skin. In our minds, our memories beats the pulse of history. Not mysterious finally, available finally because you make it, own it, it's you. If you care to listen. Learn to listen. Read through the window, the mirror of yourself. Tell it.

The way you've learned to see yourself in your father or mother. Or they can retrace in you what's made them.

The South was a winnowing for African people. The second blow of a double whammy delivered by Europeans. Test of mind after a test of body. Think of medieval trials by ordeal. Think of the Middle Passage—capture in African wars, forced marches to the coast, confinement in barracoons, crossing the Atlantic packed spoon-fashion in the holds of ships in unimaginably cruel, deadly conditions, sold into perpetual slavery—as a brutal threshing of the physically weak, and then the South as a test just as brutal for the mind.

I recall the archetypical scene of German officers in their greatcoats and shining boots processing long lines of Jews stumbling from trains that have transported them from every corner of Europe to the death camps. Some refugees would be directed by their captors to the right, some to the left. One direction meant immediate gassing and cremation, the other a living death of near starvation, unremitting hard labor in concentration-camp factories. A strong body was openers, served as your ticket to hell.

It qualified you to undergo the next trial, the mind's struggle to survive in spite of the body's imprisonment, suffering, degradation. Its theft, appropriation. Minute by minute, day by day, each prisoner chose to live or die. The burden of choice, the final selection occurs in the mind. They could decide to own you, house you, feed you enough to keep you alive. Yours to determine what choices their choices leave you.

The underground history of the camps must be remembered, written, and celebrated. The story of how strength of mind, individual and collective, altered the genocidal master plan, how the horror that destroyed so many could be transformed into a rite of passage for some, then for a people, a nation.

Yes. I want to consult the record. Learn facts, the official documentary evidence, witness, proof. Simultaneously I must not neglect the many other ways the past speaks. Through my father's voice, for instance. His hands. His eyes. Me. Sooner or later I get to myself. Another way my father speaks. To me. Through me.

It's not simply a matter of things happening again and again. That's not the burden of our personal and collective history. It's that these things never stop. Certain unexamined assumptions about "race" and color continue. The idea of "again" or "oh no, not again," is deceptive because it mixes good news with the bad. "Again" dilutes the horror, the truth of the workings of the paradigm of race. "Again" suggests something happened once, stopped, disappeared, and then reappears. Which implies *absence*, downtime, nonexistence of whatever phenomenon we greet with "shit, here it comes again." A serial killer or child molester or drug addict don't exactly stop being what they are between crimes. They just ain't doing their thing at particular moments. Clearly, to understand or treat such serious problems our focus must be enlarged far beyond moments of dramatic explosion to identify patterns, anticipate eruptions, seek root causes and means of prevention.

Yet we address white prejudice and violence directed at black people as a series of unfortunate instances, deviancy from an enlightened norm. We complain because outbreaks of urban violence are demoralizingly predictable and bloody, but resist the reality staring us in the face: the problem never goes away. And we ain't talking here about middle-class angst cause no taxis stop for your black ass in Rockefeller Center. Nor existential maundering when you ride the commuter train in from Scarsdale and the only seat white people ain't occupying is the one next to your brown ass. All that's part of the problem, but the bedrock issue raised by the paradigm of race, the question focused painfully, precisely, acutely by the experience of America's indigenous native peoples, from the massacre at Tenochtitlán to the massacre at Wounded Knee, is whether you can be someone other than a white person in this society and stay healthy, stay alive.

We respond vigorously to lynchings or urban riots, attack blatant symptoms instead of acknowledging, dealing with the constant, withering, pervasive presence of the paradigm of race. After a monumental episode of "urban unrest" a commission is appointed and the commission report inevitably advocates a long view, a broadbased approach to systematically reverse the effects of decades of injustice and inequality. For a day the report is news, for a few months or a year its recommendations may be desultorily, grudgingly implemented in a barebones fashion. Then the report's buried till the next riot, when it's dusted off, rewritten slightly to fit the new city, filed again. Read one, you've read them all. Postscript, prescription, prediction.

PLEASANT MANNERS, AMIABLE SOCIABILITY, FOLKSY charm, public access everywhere for blacks and whites, a black sheriff on the courthouse steps in Abbeville, land for sale to anyone who has the dough. I benefit from this new dispensation of southern hospitality, this southern version of northern accommodation, this new regional identity arisen from the ashes of cracker meanness, rebel aggression, aristocratic privilege, arrogant white supremacy, bald, unflinching, murderous force—Anthony Crawford, prosperous black landowner and farmer, dragged down the main street of Abbeville, beaten, and lynched by a mob in October 1916, because he dared to curse a white merchant who attempted to cheat him.

Isn't it ungenerous for a guest who's being served a delicious meal to peek under the tablecloth for crumbs, search for ancient bloodstains on the floor. How long? How long? What's the point of holding a grudge? How long can a person, a region be expected to pay for former misdeeds? Signs of progress are conspicuous, substantial. Things aren't perfect in the New South. But they aren't perfect anywhere. Handshakes, smiles, the intimacy of shared schools, libraries, courthouses, restrooms, restaurants, motels. Even dancing together in public and doing together in the dark what everybody knows happens if people drink and boogie together in nightclubs. What youall looking for, the black male clerk and white female ask when my father and I inquire about a place in Greenwood other than the Holiday Inn lounge where we might sit down and enjoy a drink. There's black clubs and white clubs and mixed. No problem with youall going in just about any of them. Depends what youall looking for.

Why quibble? Why not take things at face value? Be grateful for unsolicited, above-and-beyond-the-call-of-duty helpfulness and attentiveness received from ladies in the probate office, courthouse, the libraries. Pay attention to the health of the forest, not the inevitable stunted trees, dead trees, bare spots, stumps.

Am I a traitor, ungenerous and ungrateful, the very opposite of my hosts? I think such thoughts. See myself as duplicitous, two-faced. Sucking up to people, allowing them, encouraging them to be nice to me. Reciprocating niceness even as I indulge it. Amazed (appalled?) how well we play the game of cordiality, the good-spirited give-and-take. Wondering always what's really at stake. My behavior unnatural because I'm also testing the waters. Like a critic compiling a restaurant guide, my notebook and my plan must stay hidden in my pocket. I can't reveal my identity without biasing the experiment.

But it's biased anyway as I tabulate, keep score in my head what I can't jot in my book till later. I must be dishonest to some degree till the experiment ends, until I've stolen enough secrets. Betrayal inherent in the false premises of the relationships I establish. It's true and not true I'm a tourist with his daddy come south to search for family roots.

Who's shucking who? Is it really a one-way street— me the dissembler, my southern hosts the dupes? Could the changes I observe really be as drastic, as swift and final as they seem? Could the turnaround really have been as easy as it appears, the black-white divide like some terrible pestilence, killing, afflicting tens of thousands for centuries then a cure discovered, a vaccine, and most people are inoculated. One generation and the bad old days just a bad old memory.

I don't believe it. The paradigm of race wasn't an illness plaguing society, it was the engine creating and sustaining a particular way of life. A physician granted license to employ any means necessary, even the extreme of amputating infected parts of post–Civil War American society, a surgeon grimly determined to succeed, wouldn't have known where to make his first incision. The disease, in the form of the paradigm of race, was everywhere. Corruption would have been present during gestation, even at the point of conception, the child's fate enmeshed within the tangled sexual, racial politics of coupling, legitimacy, heredity, property, concubinage, male dominance, white supremacy, etc., etc.

Were human beings capable of undoing hundreds of

years of history virtually overnight? Maybe. If they weren't, but were trying damned hard and succeeding pretty well, maybe, if I could believe the evidence of my eyes and ears in Greenwood, South Carolina, and its environs in October 1992, then more power. Wasn't that good enough? Why knock it? Go with the progressive flow. Be grateful. Encourage what seems to be the good intentions of the good-hearted.

Yes. If the good intentions are rooted in a desire to tell the truth, to change fundamental assumptions, undo wrongs, clean the slate, start over again from as close to scratch as people can bear.

IN THE BOOKSHOP OFF THE TOWN SQUARE OF ABBEVILLE I had found none of my books. I might have attributed this shutout to the shadow of the Confederate monument in the plaza at the square's center, except more often than not, Yankee or Confederate, east or west, most bookshops didn't stock my stuff. What was unusual was the owner's regret after I identified myself as a writer with roots in the region, her admission that she wasn't familiar with my work, her assurance she'd remedy what she declared to be an unfortunate, even embarrassing oversight. She also offered to call her friend, a former professor of history at a local college who happened to be the author of a book about Abbeville, and enlist his assistance in the project that had brought my father and myself to town. Her kindness and generosity in introducing the man, his book, sharing her extensive library of local lore—books, maps, pamphlets, reprints, catalogues—were matched by the retired professor's enthusiastic response to her suggestion. Over the course of a few days he taught me in hours what might have taken me weeks to sort out on my own. I learned where and how to use some of the research materials he'd spent a good part of his life poring over. Bowie Lomax epitomized, without being stuffy, condescending, or boring, the English ideal of country gentleman and scholar. Retaining in his manner a bit of the inspired amateur, leavened with an academic's discipline and fussiness, he animated Abbeville with stories and facts. As I strolled around the square with him, literally, or in the tales he narrated while we shared a meal, every building, tree, crossroads, possessed a soul, a life history to be gleaned if you acquainted yourself with its special language. The imagination of Bowie Lomax moved in Great Time, past, present, and future simultaneously.

I'd enjoyed his company, benefitted incalculably from his patient tutelage, his stores of information as he conveyed to me the mysteries and mechanics of using Platt books, indexes, cartridge-case-like boxes of wills that had recorded property transactions in the county since before the Revolutionary War. I was grateful, even fond of this elderly man who shared himself, his insights and craft, so unreservedly with a stranger, and that's why I was surprised, shocked even, by the ice-cold wave of anger, the fury compressed into one of those if-looks-could-kill looks I found myself flashing down at the back of his thin, freckled bald skull.

From my perch on a ladder as Bowie Lomax read their serial numbers from a king-sized ledger, I was passing down metal boxes stuffed with ancient wills, letters, bills of sale, itemized appraisals of real estate and personal property that were required to legally convey wealth from the dead hand to the living. While the professor led me through the process of unearthing our shared past, my father sat outside the courthouse, basking in the sun on a bench in the restored square of Abbeville. The unanticipated glare of pure animosity had a lot to do with my father, I'm sure. He was about the same age as Bowie Lomax, as smart, as curious and engaging. Yet, because of his color, my father had been denied the prospects, the possibilities that had enriched the career and life of the white man below me.

Quickly, I realized I felt no desire to actually harm Bowie Lomax, but damage had been done. A silent apology issued from me almost simultaneous with the explosion of hostility. Nothing personal. Nothing about you, my new friend.

However, the urge to strike, to destroy, wasn't totally abstract, either. It was Professor Lomax's skull I had envisioned shattering, spilling all its learning, its intimate knowledge of these deeds that transferred in the same "livestock" column as cows, horses, and mules, the bodies of my ancestors from one white owner to another. Hadn't the historian's career been one more mode of appropriation and exploitation of my father's bones, the pearls that were his eyes. Didn't mastery of Abbeville's history, the power and privilege to tell my father's story, follow from the original sin of slavery that stole, then silenced, my father's voice. The professor was a bona fide expert. He'd earned a living studying, passing on, institutionalizing what he knew about us, including how we were bought and sold, how a region flourished based upon trafficking in human souls. Not only flourished, but attempted to legitimize and preserve its prerogatives for all the world to see with these crumbling pieces of paper we were disinterring.

I wanted the room to disappear, the hardy, vital old man to disappear, every vestige of the complacent, unrepentant reality of slavery to be scoured from the earth. My rage was not meant for my companion in that musty room crammed wall to wall, floor to ceiling, with decaying documents. What I wanted was another chance for my father. I wanted this air cleared for a different world, not so my father would be Bowie Lomax, not so Bowie Lomax would be struck down and made to suffer for the crimes of his fathers. I didn't know what kind of world, what kind of life I wished for my father or the professor or what they might wish for themselves. What should come next is always imponderable, always problematic, but I knew in that moment my anger flashed we had not severed ourselves from a version of history that had made the lives of my black father and this white man so separate, so distant, yet so intimately intertwined.

Upon a stepladder in the probate-office storage vault in Abbeville, South Carolina, I had experienced with unprecedented immediacy the fact of slavery. A grave full of chained skeletons wouldn't have been more convincing. In this room there was no denying the solid, banal, everyday business-as-usual role slavery played in America's past. Meticulously, unashamedly, the perpetrators had preserved evidence of their crimes. Given their practice the official stamp of approval. Not only did a world that once had been, shove its reality into my face, these documents also confirmed how much the present, my father's life, mine, yours, are still being determined by the presumption of white over black inscribed in them.

MY FATHER COULDN'T BELIEVE THE RECEPTION WE were receiving. After two or three days his skepticism and suspicion weren't totally allayed, yet he'd learned to relax around southern white people, gotten used to the atmosphere of casual acceptance. Unexpected and inexplicable as this welcome seemed to him, I think he remained slightly shocked he was enjoying himself as much as he was.

His last, direct experience of the South had been in the 1940s, as a soldier stationed at various army bases in South Carolina. Many mornings when the troops were mustered for roll call, white citizens from nearby towns would stand side by side with the white officers of my father's all-black unit to pick out soldiers the civilians accused of causing trouble off the base. The accused were automatically guilty. MPs would march them off for a term of forced, unpaid labor on local farms or road gangs or in the businesses of the burghers who'd been accuser, jury, and judge. Everybody on the base, black, white, enlisted men, officers, understood the drill. No one did anything to stop it. Community service southern-style. You weren't punished because you were guilty but because you were black. Color qualified you. Lynch law still ruled. To further insure good public relations between colored soldiers and local white citizens, firing pins were removed from the rifles of black troops and locked up by the white officers. My father and the other men in the unit were even forbidden to carry pocketknives. The army restricted black men to the same menial jobs that were their portion in civilian life, with the added insult and humiliation of being compelled to learn to do these jobs the army way.

Talk about a hardheaded, stubborn crew of men, my father said. You could tell those mule-head Negroes twenty times a day to do a thing a certain way and soon as you turned your back, they'd do it their way. They didn't like machines. Used to moving everything by hand. The heaviest boxes and crates. They'd muscle them. A bunch of them get around a load weighed two tons and they'd tip it on edge and muscle it side to side. Slide it along when they couldn't get it up. Rock it back and forth and wouldn't care one bit what's inside.

I'd show them how to operate the crane. How to lift the load and get the pulley rope under it and fasten the hooks. Steady the load, balance it so it doesn't swing when it rises. They'd stand there like they're listening then go and do it their way. I had to fight them with my

fists. Knock sense into their nappy heads. Take ringlead-
ers, the toughest ones, out behind the barracks. Okay.
Let's settle this shit. You whip me, you can do it your
way. I win and you do what I say. I'm not the sarge now.
Forget the army now. It's man to man. Just you and me.

Many a time I had to take one of them back behind
the barracks. I was young and strong as a bull and knew
how to box. They were strong, too. Strong, strong guys
and tough. Pow. Punch them in the head, it would be
like running your fist against a brick wall. They'd go
down, but they'd stagger right back up for more. Tough
and stubborn. Really have to hurt them before they'd
quit. But your father's hardheaded too. The men kinda
figured out finally I was just as stubborn and tough as
them. And I'd fight in a minute. They understood after
a while I meant what I said. You can push me and I'll
give a little bit. Push me the tiniest, tiniest speck more
and, No. Huh-uh. I'm not budging. Learned that from
Grandpa. Your other grandfather, your mother's daddy,
John French, the same kind of man. Reasonable man till
you push just a little too far. Then look out.

My crew learned to go along to get along when I gave
orders. Still, had to watch them like a hawk. Sneak off
and do things their way soon's I turned my back. Catch
them manhandling something should have been on the
forklift. Wasn't anything I could do sometimes. Just wring
my hands and wonder what their heads made of.

They weren't stupid. Huh-uh. No indeed. Far from it.
Just stubborn. Stubborn streak a mile long. They had a
way of doing things and didn't like anybody coming

along telling them to do it different. Specially somebody like me, who wasn't from around here.

They were smart. Real intelligent about life. You'd think they couldn't do a job without using the equipment, but they'd figure out a way. "G'wan, Sarge, we done got this handled." Smart and proud. Give them enough time and they'd figure a way. You couldn't believe a person could lift what they lifted. Slowly but surely they'd get it done.

Trouble was we didn't have all the time in the world. Couldn't get them to hurry. No way. Scoot a container ten feet, they're ready to rest awhile, stand around and smoke, shoot the breeze. Ships lined up in the harbor from here to the Philippines and more on the way. They couldn't care less. Same slow pace, same slow molasses way. Hey, fellas. A war's going on. "War have to wait awhile, Sarge, till I come back from over there behind that buildin."

Me and a few fellas from Homewood the only guys from the North. Rest of them stone South Carolina country boys. Built stocky, thick, and wide like Daddy. Dark brown-skinned like him, too. They could have all been brothers. Never been anywhere but country. Slow walking, slow talking. I was something strange to them. Couldn't understand me when I talked fast. Or claimed they couldn't. Damn sure couldn't understand them when they got off in that Geechee-Geechee. None of them could write. "Sarge. Hey, my man, Sarge." Put something special in the "sarge" when they wanted something. Wasn't really a sergeant. Squad leader really. "*Sarge*, I got this letter here. Can't make it out." Reach down in his pocket where he's kept it all neatly folded up. "Here, *Sarge.*"

Then they'd have the nerve to bad-mouth me every chance they got for being from up north. Asking me why I talk white-folks funny. Tease me. Then, one come creeping around with a letter hot in his hand.

Set in their ways. Couldn't admit I might know something they'd be better off if they knew. They'd go ahead and learn how to drive the machines. They'd do it to get along, do it if somebody's watching. Don't keep your eye on them you know they're back to the old way, their way.

Have to stay on their backs all the time. And one would try me every now and then, just to see if I was still serious. All right. You refuse to do what I say. Okay. C'mon back behind the barracks. We'll have a little talk. They were like little kids. Need a forget-me-not every so often. We were all kids really, when you come to think about it. Nineteen, twenty years old at most. Me and my buddies from Homewood. The South Carolina boys. They didn't like us and we didn't like them. Stayed out of each other's way. All of us just kids growing up during a war, trying to make sense of what they had us doing.

THE WORLD SERIES, TORONTO VERSUS ATLANTA— small version of the world if you thought about it— on TV in the Greenwood restaurant where my father,

Littleman, and I drank beer and ordered combo platters of fried seafood.

I don't think anybody minded what turned out to be a long wait for our meals. Hungry as I was, I hardly noticed time passing. Littleman and my father are back in Pittsburgh, picking up where they left off thirty years or so before. Familiar names of streets and places lace their reminiscences. Wylie Avenue. The Musicians Club. Crawford Grill. The corner of Frankstown and Homewood. Birdy Dunlap's Hurricane. Littleman asks after a few family members, satisfies himself they're still around, still okay, not pressing for more, curiously uncurious till I begin to understand how unwelcoming the Pittsburgh branch of the family, my mother's side of it anyway, where most socializing was instigated, might have been to a newcomer from South Carolina. My father had run into Littleman out in the street, work places, night places, men places. Unless Littleman happened to be driving my grandfather, and Grandpa himself only an occasional participant in our get-togethers, I couldn't remember Littleman turning up on his own at any family gathering. Even when he chauffeured my grandfather, he'd drop him off, return later. Was Littleman shy? Or my memory poor? Or did we ignore him, all of us still mired in the pathologies of color and class imposed on black people we then imposed on each other?

My mother, her siblings, her father and mother, John and Freeda French, could have passed for white. Fair skin, Caucasian features, straight hair (except John French, who'd lost all his prematurely). John French couldn't have passed for long, anyway. Not once he opened his mouth. His color showed in his Culpepper, West Virginia, speech and ways, his high disdain and arrogance and impatience anytime color intruded on how he chose to live his life or how someone else chose to treat him. My grandmother, Freeda, who took part of me away when she died, never much liked or trusted, with a few special exceptions, dark-skinned people. When hordes of dark southern folks emigrated during the early 1900s to find work in Pittsburgh's mills, she saw them as a threat to the live-and-let-live, mellow détente the Frenches and other early, predominately light-skinned Homewood residents had achieved with their Italian neighbors. Had Littleman been a late victim of the residue of this prejudice and suspicion?

I couldn't ask. Didn't. Apologized to him instead. Not out loud. I couldn't have expressed the complexity of my reaction, my regret at lost opportunities, cruelty, how they continue to cripple us, personally, collectively, a legacy of evil and unkindness with an apparently inexhaustible capacity to mutate and proliferate into ugly, new forms. Nobody was to blame. Everybody. When I was a kid I'd refused to go south with my father's father. When the South had come to Pittsburgh, perhaps one side of our family had refused it. A nasty possibility to consider, especially now, experiencing Littleman's generosity, his availability, how much he knew, how much I needed to know things only he could tell me.

When our platters finally were delivered, heaped with

brown, deep-fat-fried nuggets, strips, spirals, spheres, and planks, nobody could say for sure what variety of seafood lay hidden within each thickly crusted shape, and nobody except me came close to finishing their order.

I don't recall who won the ball game. Patrons at the bar, up two steps, partitioned from the dining area by a chest-high wall, expressed their regional loyalties vociferously. One Toronto fan, suicidal or drunk, a good ole buddy of everybody rooting for Atlanta or spoilsport or outside agitator or compound of all the above, was keeping things stirred up, bad-mouthing and signifying, his cheers and hoots perversely contrapuntal to the chorus of Atlanta fans. His life was threatened. Somebody promised to cut off his tongue and pecker if Atlanta lost. He was ordered to leave the premises more than once. The crowd tormented, blamed, teased him as Atlanta's fortunes waxed and waned.

I didn't mind the white guys at the bar heating up, as long as they stayed put. They seemed to be enjoying themselves, everything was cool, but I couldn't help feeling I might be challenged any instant. A few other black patrons were in the restaurant, but we were a decided minority. The combination of sports, liquor, young men engaged in loud talk and macho posturing doesn't bode well for race relations anywhere. And there I sat, on unfamiliar turf in the deep deep South, my northern, city instincts probably a handicap if it came down to gauging the meaning of a challenge, responding appropriately, calculating potential consequences.

Did it help or not to remember my father, Littleman,

and I weren't young men? Wouldn't be natural targets or irritants because we were just harmless old black guys sipping beer and munching fried fish.

Well, the fact the guys at the bar might not consider us worthy of a punch-up tightened my jaws. Littleman might be beyond his fighting prime, but he still appeared solid enough to hold his own. No doubt Edgar could rock 'n' roll. A legend in his time. Believe it or not we'd fought a common opponent. Both of us had faced Paul Vaughn, a feared street fighter from Garfield, known all over Pittsburgh for his heavy-handed one-punch knock-outs and bar-clearing ferocity. My father had told me his match with Vaughn had started out friendly. Guys at the municipal garage trash talking. Hey, Vaughn. You think you're bad. Well, Wideman over there. He could go. Bet he still can go. Get outta here. I don't be messing with no old man. Who you calling old, youngblood?

Started like that. Just funning. Circling, popping jabs in the air, a little openhanded cuffing, plenty space and time to duck, flurries for show, not go. People egging them on till somebody smacked somebody a little harder than necessary. Maybe to make a point, maybe not. Hands up then, blocking, bobbing, countering. Quicker. Pop. Pop. Leaning in, snapping punches faster, harder. A blow landed that's far from a tap. Fists closed. Curling. Measuring. Follow through and drive. You land one, get clipped by one you'd know it now. Not play now. You could get hurt out there. The voices in the circle lower, guttural, breathing rhythmed to the fighters'. Not coming to blows really. Nobody determined to score but far past

the edge of playfulness so anybody watching knew this
was not about fun and games but dangerous men who
could and would, if provoked, break each other up. Winner or loser, too close to call.

My father as an old head went that far with the new
devil on the block, and I duked with Paul Vaughn inside
the China Gate, then rolled around on the pavement
with him, onto the trolley tracks, till people pulled us off
one another. Vaughn a bouncer then, old tiger whose rep
mean enough to keep peace most of the time without
making war, and me fresh out of high school on my way
to college, too dumb to know or care who was standing
between me and something I wanted. Fuck you. Get it
on. Too drunk that night to know it was Paul Vaughn I
was fighting, didn't know till somebody told me next day
after my father had bailed me out of jail.

Old macho dusky disc spinning in my head so it probably wouldn't have required much of a challenge to get a
rise out of me. Fortunately, all the action, the combat,
was contained on the TV screen and inside my head. My
dad and I, back to back, turning the joint out. Pow. Pow.
Blam. Dudes falling out, carried out. How you doing, old
man? I'm fine, how you? Blam.

Yo. Pops. Soon's we finish dispatching these chumps,
how about you and me, one on one, mano a mano for
King of the Hill.

Why not?

Why not, indeed.

Imaginary or not, the danger I'd placed us in spiced
the evening for me. The adrenaline was flowing. I drank

more beer, consumed more fish than I would have otherwise. Along with the silliness, something rich and good about being with men of my family. Another kind of spice, a mellow, simple contentment arising from this meal together, a ball game, this serendipitous reunion in South Carolina. Knowing we were connected, knowing what it cost in time and blood was like savoring a delicious secret. Somehow in spite of terrible odds our ancestors had managed to survive. Not only survive, but to cache in a cave on a mountaintop a treasure, our past, our history, the inheritance we held in common. And the treasure was bountiful, there was more than enough for each of us and generations to come. We could draw from it whenever we needed it. A family. No competition, no favorites. Enough love for everybody. What had made us, delivered us to this moment could be celebrated, and would celebrate us for as long as we remembered where we came from, what joined us. Like the vital fluid of our blood, the stories of our fathers and mothers were gifts. A chance, an opportunity to create life. Life as simple and full as this coming together to talk and relax and make sense or nonsense, whatever.

His daddy and my mama was sister and brother. Matty my mama's name. Then there was Baker and Tatum we called Uncle Sonny and Uncle Foster. Josie she was the onliest other sister. Aunt Josie we call her.

James described the Reverend Tatum W. Wideman's one-horse buggy. His wife Mary, never seen outdoors without a covering on her head, riding next to the Reverend on the buggy seat. He remembers a big house, five or six rooms owned by a white man the Reverend rented from.

No. I never heared nobody say nothing about the old man's daddy. Not a name nor nothing else. Now these days been a long while back. Might have heard somebody say his name, but it's long gone now. See, Granddaddy Tatum a pretty old man by the time I remembers him. Pretty old hisself so his daddy hardly be around. Know what I mean. You say you heard it was Jordan. Jordan, you say.

On Tatum Wideman's death certificate: *Father—Jordan Wideman. Mother—unknown.*

Hmmmm. You knows the Reverend's buried right out there in Lil Zion cemetery. Right in front the church. Him and Grandmother Mary both. Sam Wideman, too. Lotta Widemans out to Lil Zion and Mount Zion, too, I reckon. Can't miss the old man's tombstone. Right in front the church. Name on it big as life.

Ball game's not over when we leave. Miss Gladys never showed up. She will the next day, along with a girl friend who wants to meet my daddy. And that's another story, so now Littleman rides back with us to the motel where he left his car. The night's chilly. A clear, starry night above the yellowish glow of parking-lot lights. In his puffy jacket Littleman looks like he might still be good for a three-round prelim.

Youall take care now.

I watch him slide behind the wheel. My father's behind

me, in a sheltered spot between two wings of the building, the overhang of the second-floor walkway connecting them.

Red taillights of Littleman's Camaro wink on, the motor turns over. I wonder why I thought it would be hot down here in South Carolina, short-sleeve, sitting-by-the-pool hot. It might be warmer back in New England if the Indian summer I'd left hadn't slunk, heel-toe away.

It would be even colder in the morning at Lil Zion, frost silvering the grass and weeds, crunching like that crusty fish, we'd have to tromp through to reach the graves.

Picking Up My Father
at the Springfield Station

For SOME ABSURD SET OF REASONS MY FATHER WAS LEFT behind. Three cars en route from Pittsburgh to Amherst for the wedding, but for various obvious and some not as obvious reasons, no room for him. He was seventy-two and still unyielding as stone, but not quite as hard and strong as stone anymore, though he would fight you or anybody else in a minute, fight any person or circumstance that suggested he'd lost one speck of the power supporting his right to be respected and treated like a man. So I knew the others had hurt him deeply, even if unintentionally, by not figuring a way to include him in one of the vehicles caravaning the family from Pittsburgh to Amherst, Massachusetts, for the wedding of his grandson, my son, Danny.

Left behind, the image of powerlessness, alone, broke, stuck in Pittsburgh. At the last minute his sister, my Aunt Catherine, knowing how hurt he was, knowing he'd never ask for help, knowing how much the trip meant to him and how impossible it is for him to admit or share what he feels, knowing he probably contributed to the mix-up by waiting for people to contact him rather than getting in touch with them and participating in planning the arrangements, exasperated as she'd always been at her brother's male pride and stubbornness—Why didn't you just pick up the phone, Edgar, and tell somebody you needed a ride?—knowing all this she still considered leaving him sitting there feeling sorry for himself to teach him a lesson, a lesson he deserved since he always brought this kind of trouble down on other people's heads as well as his own. Catherine, in spite of copious reasons for abandoning him to a richly deserved fate, relented at the last minute and handed him money for a train, calling it, to salvage his pride, a loan.

Amtrak took sixteen hours for the 550-mile trip. Only one set of connections could get him to the festivities in time (Train #42, Pittsburgh to New York; #654, New York to Springfield, Massachussetts). The Springfield station was thirty miles from my home in Amherst, and that's why I found myself driving at 1:00 in the morning of the eve of my son's wedding to meet my father's 2:30 A.M. train.

Actually everything was working out just fine. An hour earlier I'd settled my sister Tish, her husband, and youngest daughter in a motel across the Calvin Coolidge Bridge on the outskirts of Amherst. Since departing Pittsburgh they'd been on the road twelve hours. My mother, the other passenger in the car, had been deposited to stay at my home before I led Tish, Baron, and Tunisia to the grubby little place that was the best I could find at the last minute on this busy Labor Day, county-fair, horse-show, students-returning-to-the-five-local-colleges weekend. The wedding and myriad of nuts-and-bolts arrangements it required had been postponed once, remained in an on-again, off-again limbo while we waited for the U.S. Immigration and Naturalization Service to sort out their fears and suspicions of Maimuna Mahdi, my prospective daughter-in-law, her Sierra Leone passport, Muslim name and religion. Finally INS said yes, so the wedding was on again with everybody involved—from Africa, Europe, and North America—scrambling to make it right.

The Country Inn was staffed by Indian immigrants. A night clerk with skin many shades darker than mine greeted us warily, reluctantly, close enough to rude to tighten my jaws. Evidently he was upset by the prospect of brown people checking in and more brown people on their way to occupy the rooms I'd reserved over the phone. Smacking him or rapping with him until we both understood the history, the irony of this moment were equally impractical options, so I stayed cool. His attitude softened when I produced a gold MasterCard and a UMass faculty ID. It's those people drive over from

Holyoke and Springfield. I am cleaning rooms all the day after those people. Not nice people. Not like you. Bad. Bad.

Nearly one before business at the motel completed— Tish and family in their room, the other reserved rooms inspected, bill prepaid. The night clerk informs me he's also the owner, yet here he is pulling the graveyard shift because the only way to get ahead in this country is hard work. Work. Work. All the time work. He wags his small, tar-capped head. Fingers delicate as a child's tap, tap the tabletop serving as a counter. Why don't those Springfield people and Holyoke people work. I don't understand those people.

He offers me a soda from a padlocked cooler in the lobby that's also his office. Barely veiled hostility has given way to a kind of unctuous, fawning attentiveness. After all, I'm spending lots of money, I speak, dress differently than the ones who drive over here to party on weekends, so maybe I'm not really like them. He's up in my face, looking for approval because he's able and willing to distinguish me from the others and treat me now, suddenly, as if I'm an old buddy.

I see him or the wife I imagine for him or the daughter who is a smaller, identical version of the mother, colorful cylinder of sari, same long black, black braid, on hands and knees trying to scrub Ripple from one of the green carpets. I decline the soft drink anyway.

Up past my bedtime but the Country Inn right off I-91, on the way to Springfield, so everything working out just fine. When I hit the interstate and punch open windows and sunroof, the rush of night air is a bracing second wind. Jazz wings in from far away, the signal weak, a little staticky, but cooking once I pump the volume. Exhausted from a couple days of last-minute preparations for the wedding, but up on my toes now, sprinting the gun lap. My Pittsburgh family beginning to gather in this pretty New England place almost none of them had visited before, the first load safe, tucked away for the night and me with only one more chore, picking up my father at the Springfield station, delivering him to the Country Inn, and then I could hit the bed, and bed, no matter how long or short a stay, sweet light at the end of the tunnel.

I'd been dreading the meeting with my father. More than the usual worry about finding something to talk about, the usual uneasiness about coming face to face with a man I loved who was also a stranger. Dread this time because I knew he'd be hurt and angry beyond words. More unsaid words piling up between us. Words always too clumsy to form the questions I needed him to answer. Questions on hold for years, years during which I seldom saw my father, years thickening the silence.

Do you wear a mask of not caring in order to protect yourself, or are you simply ice-cold or do you post yourself at the switch of your feelings, eternal vigilance the price you pay so you're able to turn them off and on at will.

I was betting he'd greet me wearing the armor of his indifference. See, they didn't hurt me. Nothing can hurt me. Living proof once more that only fools or babies let

down their guard, that wise men keep themselves sheltered against the worst because the worst is always possible, always happening, a disease that family, friends, the
ones closest to you carry, and you better not ever allow
them to get too close. You could not escape bad news,
but you could keep your distance, stay prepared for the
worst.

I'd never learned how to behave when I encountered
my father's hardness. What I dread about it most is its
power to shut me down. Double-distanced. If he refuses
to reach out to me, why in the hell should I reach out for
him or anybody else? Why shouldn't I bury my feelings,
too? Wasn't that what he'd taught me? His determination
to keep his distance, his style of coming closer and turning away simultaneously, the attractive spin his charm
put on evasion, denial. Wasn't I his son in all this, his
twin mirrored on the glass wall separating us when we
spoke? Wasn't I becoming him when I made certain my
answers to questions never left me unprotected? What
I dreaded a sure thing, an already accomplished fact: I
couldn't win with my father for losing, the part of him I
dreaded also the deepest bond.

Cool breeze flying in the windows flushed out stale
air. Scat singing out loud, I kicked back in the bucket
seat, pulled on the music like a new suit of clothes, shaking my shoulders, scooting my behind up and back and
sideways, all my body parts posing, dancing, to show off
the fine garment they sported.

A spy camera stationed on a satellite might have
picked up through its infrared laser telescopic lens a

bruise-purple and grayish cloud rising from my Volvo's open sunroof. Bad air out, good air in, just like old Satchmo sang. Wasn't I cruising down the freest place in America, the highway at night? Warp speed across an unexplored galaxy. Nothing visible but other car lights, each pair with its private gravity and varieties of life, separated absolutely from every other pair, even though the fickleness of perception causes some stars to loom, a single burst of light engulfing you as they crest the blackness, leap past inches away.

Dread receded, crawled into the back seat for a nap. I can't recall the tunes playing that night on I-91, but they were the right ones, they did the trick. Coltrane or Smokey and the Miracles or the Soul Stirrers or Big Bill Broonzy or Miles. You can hear it, can't you, whether I name the tunes or not. Music free as the night highway.

Not that easy, of course. Dread sleeping in the back seat, but didn't the past lead the future by the nose? Would I become my father one day? Shouldn't I be prepared to live his way, heed the lessons of his life I tried to resist, deny?

On one of my trips to Pittsburgh, he'd said: See. For once in my life I wanted to be able to do the things I wanted to do. Not worry about everybody and everything the way your mother does. Worry worry worry. I couldn't worry every minute of every day the way she does. Huh-uh. I needed some time just to enjoy life. Do what I wanted to do before I got too old and helpless.

He'd been frowning. Perhaps from the effort of saying the words, turning over memories they freed. Both of us very aware of the consequences of his decision to leave his family, the complicated story he'd pared down to a few simple words. *Worry* included me, my mother, sister, and brothers. We were the flesh and blood stuffed into the words. We had prevented him from enjoying a life of his own. A man with children myself the first time my father had acknowledged, let alone tried to explain or apologize for deserting his family. The cost of enjoying his life, price of the ticket, had been walking out the door, leaving my mother and the rest of us. He continued to send money, as much, whenever he could, to keep us in food and clothes and a roof over our heads, but declared himself gone, on his own. His life starkly separate from ours, as clearly defined as certain jarred or foil-wrapped delicacies he ripped off from the fancy parties he served, loot he stashed in the refrigerator, *his*, our mother warned us, and we better not touch, it better be sitting right there on the shelf for your father when he gets home from work.

Not easy now to recall exactly when he did leave. My parents had lived apart more than once as I grew up. I must have been about twenty-eight when my father moved out for good. After the time I had moved out myself, for college, and grad school, the new life they promised. No babies in the house, my youngest sibling, Robby, seventeen or eighteen. So my father had stuck with us, in his fashion, for a long time. Robby remembers silence and distance between our parents for years before the end, but he also recalls Daddy on the steps of Soldiers and Sailors Hall the night of Robby's high school graduation. Yeah, he had a look on his face like, Got all you all through, I'm finished now. I can rest. When Rob remembers that night, he hears a song, *Color Me Father*, a popular song from those days that still brings tears to his eyes, corny and dumb as it was.

Difficult now to recall how I felt about his leaving, how the house changed with him not around, because I'd left the house, too, and he'd been away, in his fashion, off and on, for most of my life. He floats in and out of my recollections of growing up, like memory itself, hauntingly ambiguous, presence and absence two sides of a coin, and when you toss it to decide what really happened, it lands standing on edge.

Perhaps he had a purpose in waiting so long to speak, waiting till we'd served ourselves from an elaborate breakfast buffet and sat down together in a booth at the Waffle House out on Monroeville Road, waited till I was a father so when I listened, his words weren't only about him but about the core of ego, ambivalence, potential for betrayal, hunger for the unknown few of us ever quell completely, no matter how character or fate lead us to behave. My father passed the pepper or the half-and-half or whatever and I understood exactly what he meant. Could not blame, forgive, empathize, exonerate without implicating myself.

During our annual or semiannual visits to Pittsburgh my wife, kids, and I would stay at my mother's house. Time with my father squeezed in, a few minutes here and there, maybe. Sometimes we'd meet like bachelors, just the two of us for a drink or a meal on neutral, public ground, time borrowed from our regular lives, two men, two fathers hooking up, a funny twist on boys' night out, enjoying restaurants, bars, playing free at last while it lasted.

I wanted to be able to do the things I wanted to do. A frown had furrowed his forehead, emphasized deep, vertical lines from the wings of his nose to his chin, hingeing his mouth like a puppet's. Flesh showing its age, stretched, pouched, incised. An old man's face finally imprinting my father's flesh, but the eyes ageless, elsewhere.

His mouth worked, chewing slowly as he always did, slower and longer than anyone else at the family table. Nothing left to chew, you'd think. You'd think he's done and we'll be excused and there he goes, twisting his mouth, sucking his cheek, his tongue busy inside his jaw, the inevitable toothpick he produces from nowhere like a magician to dig out morsels his tongue couldn't budge. While he finished the final, stubborn, invisible remnants of his meal that morning in the Waffle House, a certain way he balled up one side of his face pulled the other cheek taut and reminded me of one of those maneuvers I learned as a kid watching him shave. Slipping just inside the bathroom door if he'd left it open, I'd stand behind him, quiet as the dark face in the mirror. Shaving was a movie of my father we watched together. Okay to stare, to study him in the mirror because he was staring and studying, too. The face in the mirror not really my father, it would disappear when he turned his back on it.

Sometimes what he did in front of the mirror each morning seemed like fun and games. He'd sing, splash hot water into the sink, whip up lather in a mug with his floppy-bristled shaving brush, pat on a foamy white beard, flip his straight razor open like a switchblade, peek at himself, smile, frown, lean in for close-ups till he fashioned just the face he was after. Or the mood could be strictly business, no-frills surly, just finish the job, don't draw blood. Without saying a word, he taught me. Taught the tricks of shaving, the tricks of time. My future lay enfolded within the depths of the mirror. One day I would need to do the things he did, know things he knew. Not today and not tomorrow exactly because I already knew them, had done them already. Many faces in the mirror. His. Mine. We both saw them, we both could turn away from them, but they'd be there, staring, studying when we looked again. Measuring us as we measured them. Part of being a man would be performing daily the rituals I'd learned from the screen where the image of my father's face hovered, dissolving, emerging, doubling, winking at me, ignoring me as steam rose from the sink, misted the glass.

In the din and bustle of the restaurant his mouth had worked intently in its own good time to dislodge hidden bits he needed to chew more. His heavy-lidded eyes, nearly closed, focused inward, distracted by whatever they'd fixed upon, wherever they'd landed as he recalled his decision to leave his wife and children. In that booth with his grown son could he see the place he'd glimpsed decades before when he'd decided he must break from his family. Could he visualize again the world apart he'd been seeking when he'd walked out the door of the house on Marchand Street, the house I'd left when I went off to college? What had it looked like to him, this elsewhere he was headed towards, damn the cost? Was it a world where desires could be fulfilled, where grown men could have fun? I had wanted to ask him if he remembered what his vision of his future had been. Ask him if he could describe it. Could he picture it for me now, that shimmering place men and women need to believe in, long after they know better. How had it appeared to him thirty-some years ago when he'd decided to step through the looking glass. And how did it appear that morning breaking bread together, many years having elapsed, having been what they were, what most people's lives were, if not exactly a tissue of wrack and ruin, a colossal morning-after mess, the kind he faced after serving one of those sloppy, drunken parties for white people, then had to clean up after everybody leaves, room after nasty room and you're hung over from bolting good whiskey every chance you got all night and don't know where to start, you'll never finish clearing away the mess, this is your life, and dawn cracking again while we slept at home in our beds.

Did I still want to know what he had seen? To be inside him peering out at a world free of the weight, the burden of me, my siblings, my mother. Was it possible to join him in that alluring, unfallen world? Son, father. Father, son. Could we meet at last as equals? Equally shorn, equally alone. Myself unborn or extinguished, out of the way, separate, not a burden to him, myself nor anyone else. Not myself. And him not himself. Both of

us free as figments of a dream. The story goes sons kill
fathers to become men, assume their rightful place in
society. The king is dead. Long live the king. Isn't the
other story also always true? Fathers slay sons.

You grow old and then you die. Fathers impart this
brutal wisdom. The father's body inscribed with messages
of change, loss, failure. One of his jobs to pass on the
message willy-nilly, one way or another. Drop it like a
bomb, leave it in a basket on the doorstep. He can't
always take you with him, but you will follow in his
footsteps.

IF YOU TURN RIGHT OUT OF THE PARKING LOT BEHIND
Mount Zion A.M.E. Church in Promised Land, South
Carolina, someone had said the road would take you past
where the Wideman place used to be. Nothing much
back in there now, he said. Don't know how long it been
since anybody living there. House stood empty awhile
but wasn't much left of it by then. Folks carried off most
of it worth anything. Kids tore down the rest. Gone now.
Maybe some them old peoples live back down there tell
you exactly where the Widemans stayed.

The road twisted and dipped a good ways before the
first houses were visible, skimpy houses separated by
marshy-looking fields, scraggly patches of woods. Too
far to walk. My father would be looking for me back at
Mount Zion, ready to be rescued from the noisy aftermath of Sunday morning services.

I pictured a clearing set back from the road, overgrown

with weeds and grass, yet still distinct, a house-and-yard-sized plot of bright green surrounded by thickets of brush and overhanging trees. Poking around over in there, I might find the grave of a household, the skeleton of a dwelling. If I wasn't careful, I might find the ancient black muck that had nearly swallowed my father seventy years before. Back in there might be bones—chicken bones, pork bones, dog bones, the ghost bones of the old vagrant woman Aunt Huldy Green. On a February night in 1923 she'd been caught in a snowstorm and lost her way. They found her dead next morning, wearing one shoe, *with a bit of old sweater tucked under her head and another rag of sweater thrown over her face,* in a cotton field just a few dozen yards from the Wideman place she'd been crawling through rows of frozen cotton stubble to reach.

I remembered that Promised Land road as I walked alone down a dusty rural track outside the Arizona State Prison Complex in Tucson. My feet were on the road, my mind elsewhere, telling me there is no Arizona, no South Carolina, there are only empty roads like this one, the same road always, going nowhere.

I was keeping myself company by singing inside my head, a gospel song pitched in my father's mellow tenor (he can sing, yes he can, the man can sing), and the song was as close as I come to praying, a kind of prayer in it because the people who had raised me, whom I loved, believed in a presence above their heads, up there in the middle of the air, invisible, all-powerful, and it was to this presence the sweetness, the yearning, the climbing of their voices were addressed, not because they expected prayer ever to be answered, but because the emptiness overwhelmed unless you believed in something out there with you, larger than your doomed, wandering self. I didn't believe in my mother and father's God so my song wasn't sent there, but I had witnessed all my life the miracle of my people's belief and the song I sang to myself, though not exactly addressed to their God, would have been hollow, impossible, would have contained no chance to sustain me without the reality of their lives that also included Him.

In spite of disbelief, a kind of prayer in the gospel song because I was mourning, drifting like my African ancestors, through a strange land, searching for some bit of something, if no more than rags from a sweater like old Huldy Green had arranged around herself before she settled down to her final sleep, some presence alive or dead with the power to release my imprisoned son, bear us across the waters home.

By then, on that walk away from steel bars, electrified fences, concertina wire, concrete bunkers, and gun towers, wishing for the basilisk's fiery stare to sweep the prison from the earth when I turned to it again, I'd read a book called *Tumult and Silence at Second Creek* and learned of refugee camps outside southern cities like Natchez, Mississippi, where, after the Civil War, newly freed slaves had gathered to die. Hordes of women, children, the infirm and elderly were stranded in these doomed encampments, exiled far enough away from the cities so the racket and stench of slow death by starvation did not worry the townsfolks' sleep. War had separated able-bodied black men from their families. No longer of any use as cannon fodder and laborers to the victorious Union, landless, superfluous in a defeated, devastated plantation economy, the men, dispersed great distances by wartime duties, wandered up and down the ruined countryside, seeking their kin, begging work, foraging provisions where there was neither welcome nor aid. Decades later, people on pleasure outings—hunters, picnickers, lovers —were still finding bones of victims who'd perished in the camps. My feet scuffed up the bone-haunted dust of their remains on the desolate road outside the prison.

I had discovered in the same book that one of the conspirators in a rebellion led by the slave Gabriel in Virginia in 1800 launched a message in a bottle that washed up many years later and was found beside a tide-water road.

dear frind—brother X will come and preach a sermont to you soon and then you may no more about this bissiness.

Darkness changes one place to another. We learn night vision, double vision. A child in a comfortable house in a comfortable neighborhood frets in her bed, unable to sleep, seeing in the darkness more than she sees in daylight, much more than she wishes to see. Consider the ancient linkage between blindness and prophecy. The sightless seers. A throbbing third eye in a wizard's forehead. Sure-handed old midwives unravel a caul from a newborn's brow; they fold and preserve the veil in a special fashion, mutter songs as they work, pray the bearer be blessed, not cursed, by second sight. Such con-tradictions, divisions, ironies cluster here, where I am, a place that is also, always, someplace else, many changing places at once. Imagine yourself making me up, being me, freeing yourself as I start to take on the weight and independence of a personality as lifelike as the one you possess, as real as the one you've deserted.

IN COLUMBIA, SOUTH CAROLINA, THE SOUTH CARO-
lina Humanities Council together with numerous other civic groups and organizations promoting art and racial harmony sponsored an exhibit of African-American fam-ily portraits dating from the nineteenth and early twenti-eth centuries. Someone had discovered an atticful or barnful of old glass photographic plates, many never be-fore developed. A time capsule, treasure trove of cultural history. Long-dead Negro faces above Edwardian collars, under bowler hats. Many-buttoned bodices, lace ruffles at neck and sleeve, bone-corseted waists, bustles, lank homespun dresses to the ground, cutaway coats, furs, farmers in jackets with abbreviated sleeves, matrons with strings of pearls; a dashing watchchain decorating a vest, elegance and grim dignity, eyes gazing out at you where you are crouched behind the camera, your face hidden under a hood as you stare back, prepare to shoot.

Some of your subjects smile, many are stiff and uncom-fortable, others challenge the camera with their confi-dence and beauty, a few somber ones stare through the artifice of picture taking, remind you of immense dis-tances they've traveled, oceans traversed, rows of cotton chopped that if linked would circle and recircle the

globe, remind you of the soul you cannot steal, the un-
crossable divide between who they are and who you are,
even as they rise up through the tray of chemicals you've
brewed to draw out their likenesses.

A gala reception at the South Carolina Historical Museum attracted hundreds, a crowd containing the largest
percentage of African-descended people that had ever
graced a museum affair. If you didn't know better, if you
ignored the photos on the walls, the slight modifications
in style from then to now at this fancy-dress event, you
might have imagined yourself at a Reconstruction Ball
during the impossible, gilded, *never again* moment when
black people mixed socially with the ruling class of
whites, controlled the South Carolina legislature, strolled
comfortably, freely in the marbled corridors of Justice.

A friend told me opening night was a smashing success. Only hitch being a sort of bewildered, wandering
unease among the black people, growing more palpable
as the evening waned and they searched fruitlessly in the
vast gallery of faces for relatives. Though the photographs had been miraculously disinterred and reproduced
with amazing clarity in spite of a smoky, ash-flecked
patina coarsening the grain of some, and though many of
the faces were achingly, dauntingly familiar, the names
of the sitters were missing. Gone. Gone. Gone. Perhaps
once during the course of the reception, a shock, a holler,
hot tears of recognition may have exploded. An elderly
guest testifying, pointing with bent-fingered, horny-
nailed, blue-gummed authority and certainty. That's her.
That's him, all right. Sure as I'm standing here. Mama

kept this very picture in her chifforobe drawer. Uncle Tatum and Uncle Foster and Uncle Baker. Them little boys you see your granddaddy's brothers. Call him Sonny and this one right here on the end she's Mattie. Aunt Mattie.

The rest of the well-dressed African-American visitors had browsed the walls and come up empty, disappointed, disconcerted. The best they could manage, a *maybe.* Maybe yes, maybe no. A braid long enough to sit on they'd heard celebrated in family stories, and here's one python-thick draped over a woman's shoulder, but many other women in the photos displayed long, Indian-straight hair, those fabled Cherokee cheekbones. The weight of too much anonymity distressed people, damp-ened spirits. The names irretrievably lost. You could guess or imagine, argue or pretend a connection with this likeness or that telltale feature, but the sobering fact was that without names, the coffle of ancestors could not be claimed. Except generally, collectively. Rather sad really, she said. I felt badly for them. All these nice people had gussied themselves up and trotted out to attend a grand family reunion. Then the guests of honor never showed. Ghosts. Like wandering through a gallery full of ghosts. Positively eerie after a while. Who were these people? Successful, middle-class blacks so disappointed and out of sorts. They couldn't say out loud what was bothering them because too many of us silly white folks buzzing around. Bizarre really. I left as soon as I decently could.

Ironically, I heard my friend's account of the exhibit's opening night while I was in Promised Land, South Carolina, with my father researching our family history. She made it sound like everyone in attendance believed they held a winning lottery ticket, one of those undercover stings where a bunch of crooks are scammed into thinking they've won some luxurious item, but when they arrive to collect, they're greeted by cops and handcuffs. I was luckier than most of the museum crowd. In our trip south I'd unearthed no family pictures, but did learn my great-grandfather's name and the name of his father, pushed back the curtain two more generations to find Tatum W. Wideman and Jordan Wideman. Later I was struck by the thought that by chance photographs of Tatum and Jordan may have found their way to Columbia and been displayed in the collection. I could have been one of the people milling about, drink in hand, canapé in mouth, frustrated, puzzled, while my ancestors, framed and mounted in a corner, shouted to get my attention.

Not long after I returned from finding the name Jordan on his son Tatum Wideman's death certificate in a public records office in South Carolina, my sister's daughter Tameka named her new baby Jordan. Too much of a coincidence to be a coincidence. One Jordan appearing at the back door while another knocks at the front. I ask Tameka why she chose the name Jordan and her answer's vague. She liked the sound of the name mostly. Huh-uh, it had nothing to do with Michael or basketball, and she's positive she had no idea in the world Jordan was the name of her great-great-great-grandfather.

One summer day three years ago I mentioned to my friend Jamal the idea of a "roots" trip to Promised Land,

South Carolina, with my father. Researching our roots but also a chance for the long talk fathers and sons seem never to get around to.

Go. Go, Jamal had said. Don't wait. I wish I could take such a journey with my father today. I wish it weren't too late now. He blinked once, slowly, a veil lowered or raised. I recognized what glistened in his eyes, turned away to the tall trees fencing one end of his backyard, the innumerable greens there, from black to the bone-pale undersides of leaves twisting, shimmering in the highest branches. I've begun crying again, I tell him.

Half a century and change old, Jamal. An old man almost and I've started crying at the drop of a hat. Me. Who never cried. Sneaky, hot tears. Hat don't even have to drop, man. See a battered, crimped-up, stringy brim, tilted just so on some old brother's knotty, scarred head. Just the sight of it perched there enough to make tears come. Embarrassing. Can't take myself no place, man. Liable to start crying like a baby.

We're on Jamal's back deck. At the edge of the woods on a perfect summer day. A red, sweat-seamed bandanna secures Jamal's coiled dreads. He'd been working in his yard earlier and had lost track of his tree-trimming, weed-chopping, island machete. My ESP told me it lay somewhere over near the woodpile, scrap-pile disorder to the left of the elaborate swing set Jamal had constructed for his daughter Maya's visits. For some reason, maybe just to prove my ESP still potent, I wanted to find the knife, restore it to Jamal.

Oh yes. Yes. I know exactly the tears you're talking

about, my brother. Damned things come all the time. Unexpectedly. Unbidden. No logic or apparent reason. A disease of late middle life, I suspect. A reservoir of tears we should have been draining all along. Them come when them want to come. Coursing down my cheeks before I realize they there.

Maya clatters across the deck in her Dutch girl clogs, hugs me, shows me her special stick. A twig split lengthwise so its insides—a whitish, fibrous sap imprinted with hieroglyphs—are exposed. The twig's marrow hard and soft like the balsa wood I'd carved, glued, and sanded into warplanes when I was Maya's age. I wished I could name the white substance for her, identify the plant from which the twig had been broken. I pressed my fingernail into the vein of stuff, cut a crude letter. See. You can write secret messages. Rub away the lines already there, like this. Now you need something hard and pointy and you can make letters, scratch your name.

Maya's long lashes are lowered as she concentrates on the stick. Then the flash of a wide-eyed grin. Her deep brown eyes are the kind which stop you in your tracks. She is a package mailed from a distant planet, fresh in this world where Jamal and I have put in between us a century's worth of years. Jamal's blood in her, but she's not of our world, not quite, not yet. In the late afternoon sunlight, under a blue sky spattered with cottony puffs of cloud, the distance beween her and us is merciful, a wonder, a marvel and then an ache as she hustles her stick into the house to find a pointy tool.

It won't really work, I'm thinking. The band of stuff in

the center will crumble. Twig will break. Think of all the failed games I've invented and tried to play. Kept me busy but never worked out the way I hoped. I'd tried this one once, writing on the dingy marrow. Seemed a good idea then, maybe now. And even if it doesn't work, so what. Maya might be amused a few minutes, stay away from the porch while Jamal finished a story she didn't need to overhear. Not yet. Not quite.

The market wasn't there, he said. Fellow who promised to buy all the cucumbers my brother could grow never returned at harvest time. My brother stuck with a field of cucumbers nobody want. Him think, Can't afford to let them go to waste. Let my cows in there. Oh Lawd. Why he think that. Cucumber plain poison to cow. Next thing he know his cows got all four feet pointing to heaven. Ones ain't lying upside down on their backs, leaning cross-eyed against the trees.

Yes, mon. Old slave-driving buckra nastiness a curse on the land. People warn my brother not to buy the white man's farm. Everybody know the terrible things happen there. But my brother covet the farm. A beautiful piece of land. Choicest on the island. If truth be told, given the chance, I might have bought it, too.

Story of the gophered farm a thread weaving in and out of the story of Jamal's broken marriage. He tilts back in his chair, shoots out two stiff arms, two stiff legs, lolls his head over the backrest, rolls his eyeballs.

Woe is me. Woe is me, my brother cry. Help me, Jesus. All him cow not dead staggering around like a bunch of sailors fulla rum.

We're both cracking up now. Jamal wipes his eyes with the back of his hand. Funny story mixes with sad one. Both are sad, both funny as he runs one into the other, his doomed marriage, his brother's doomed farm. Good intentions and high hopes, pratfalls, broken hearts.

His long, blunt fingers tap deftly, delicately, produce a single cigarette from a blue pack of Gitanes. He clamps it between two knuckles, holds it, poised, ready to light, the entire routine performed on automatic pilot, unconnected to the flow of the story, till his hand hesitates, shakes when he raises the cigarette to his mouth. A stutter as if he's remembering his vow to quit smoking, as if he's noticed the jar lid tattooed with burns that has replaced hidden ashtrays. Perhaps he's flashing on Maya. Is she in the kitchen or on her way outside again to catch him, scold him. Jamal shakes off the weight of the choice. His hand's steady as he lights up, puffs serenely as a white man who's just set free an islandful of slaves.

AFTER THE EXIT RAMP ON I-91 EAST, TO REACH THE Springfield railroad station you keep bearing right through anonymous arteries of street and road in various stages of finish. No people here, only concrete and emptiness, blowing crap. You could be on the wrong side of a backdrop whose face is painted to seem like a city. You see braces, scaffolding, steel beams, and wires jerryrigged to support the illusion of city, stuff the audience isn't supposed to notice from their seats out front. Filth and grit accumulating for years because no one cleans backstage or paints, no one needs to pretend this abandoned, litter-strewn approach to the city is anything but what it is. The scale of your surroundings is intimidatingly massive: expressway overpasses, vast, unpaved stretches of no-man's-land where streets and roads dissolve, hulking buttresses and piers of the interstate, strung with cables thick as trees. The whine, clatter, thump of wildly varying road surfaces under your tires increase the feeling of being out of control, being lost, stuck somewhere you shouldn't be, behind zebra-striped barriers or yellow police tape, a restricted zone that just might be dangerous for you or your vehicle but you missed the warning signs. Not only are you in jeopardy, but maybe you're about to crash through the façade, knock down some crucial stick propping up the immense, haphazard ugliness pretending to be a city.

Picturing myself in my car again on the way to pick up my father for the wedding, my route through the outskirts of Springfield brings me down and around to the city proper, a long, straight street in another country, with homemade shop signs in Spanish, blocks of Third World decay, citizens of many colors draped in windows, doorways, on corners, in parked cars, often with a look in their eyes that asks what you're asking—Is this the right place, how in the hell did I wind up here?

A kind of scoured openness on all sides when you reach the broad streets intersecting at the Peter Pan bus depot. The sense of claustrophobia, of being an intruder abruptly ceases. No, you aren't lost, this is the way, you didn't detour and trespass into someone else's country, these wide streets, bland, commercial buildings assure you you're still in a Massachusetts town. Through a series of lights, an underpass, then the street narrows again, the marquee of the Roxy or Imperial or Palace advertises ancient coming attractions and you signal a left turn, across oncoming traffic.

I go effortlessly to the station, imagining a daytime ride, though it was night when I picked up my father, the route perfectly reproduced except for a tiny blank spot where the name of a street I can't recall should be printed on a sign stuck to a building across the intersection where I turn to parallel on my left a high wall of sooty-faced stone blocks rising to the plateau upon which trains cross the city. The bare, white shield of sign teases me. The street name precious because it's not there.

When I turn onto this unidentifiable street, cut off from the city by a looming stone wall, it's night again. Two-thirds of the way down the long block, cabs cluster at the double glass doors of the Springfield station. Cars occupy all the metered spaces on the station side of this one-way street and stretch in an unbroken row along the side marked no parking. Cars ahead of me and cars behind, a bright-eyed parade snaking along at 1:30 in the morning. A cop car, roof light pulsing, stalls traffic till it climbs the curb at the entrance to the station. Once past this commotion, I notice red taillights of a parked car wink on. I brake. Wait for a tan compact to maneuver away from the curb, signaling the driver behind me to stay put, so I can pull up and back in, hoping I won't have to fight, kill, or be killed for this vacant slot.

As I lock up, I check out the station entrance. A man's leading two cops through the doors. In a big hurry. White-helmeted cops brandishing nightsticks. Half past one in the morning. Someone, somewhere in the station behaving badly. Somebody hurt or about to be hurt.

The night warm. I'd noticed bare arms and legs inside parked cars. At least an hour before my father's train due. Cabbies milling around the door are discussing the likelihood of being robbed. Who has been, who hasn't, a guy who got hit three times who's giving up night work even though it's the least-hassled driving and good tips.

The cops exit, casual and cocky, no civilian in tow. Their car, strobe spinning, shrugs off the sidewalk into snarled traffic, plowing a lane where there didn't seem room for one. The bright door of the station at this hour a bit like the threshold of a nightclub. A stage. A gauntlet. I hang at the periphery of the cabbies' talk, where the glow framing the entrance begins to merge with shadow. Play the game of being a regular, not only in this world, but of it. Check out the cruising cars while their occupants check me out. Let people wonder who I might be, what my job is on this street busy as high noon in the middle of the night.

When a woman wearing six-inch spike heels and a black miniskirt clatters down the sidewalk from the dark end of the street and turns, all hip-length, bouncing red pony-tail and lean, long bare legs, into the train station, I ride her wake through the doors, far enough behind to watch the cabdrivers watch her. Though none of the men close to blocking her way, each backs off a fraction of an inch as she trots by.

An elderly, brown-skinned guy with a ring of keys and a broom sits on a bench fastened to the floor just inside the door. He clears his throat and glances at another guy in coveralls, slouching nearby. Both give the young woman a swift, concentrated, head-to-toe exam. Yes, they see her. Yes, they are quite aware her Lycra top is more like a paint job with very thin paint than a piece of clothing, and yes they're aware she's nearly naked from the waist down and young and slinky sexy enough to turn most men's heads, turn most men's dicks hard if they let their dicks get hard every time some hustling ho' all skinny legs and hair and bubble of butt with most of her booty showing comes around. The men look—looking's free, ain't it?—quickly find each other's eyes again, and exchange a nod. Uh-huh. Yeah. So what, girl. Don't mean a thing. Ain't nothing to me.

The woman plugs coins into a coffee machine and gets no satisfaction. Slaps it a couple of times, turns to the man with the broom, flashes a half-frown, half-question at him. He shrugs. On duty but none of his business. She digs into her shoulder bag, finds more change, and plinks it in. Machine delivers second go-round. She bends to draw out the paper cup of coffee. Calves flex, a little quiver of thigh. Bends miraculously so she exposes no more of her behind than's already on display. Lets you know she knows you're looking, and she's in charge of what's free and what ain't. She's the show and knows that, too. Pouts at the vending machine, puckers her purple lips, blows on the cup and gingerly takes a sip. No satisfaction. She wrinkles her nose. With her free hand she pats and smooths the nothing she's wearing, tosses the rope of fake red hair over one shoulder, pumps up on spike heels, and in a tap-tappety-tap volley she's back out on the street.

No sign of a disturbance the brace of cops and civilian had been chasing. Nowhere for anybody to hide in the tiny waiting room. One door straight ahead, another to the left, lead to the tracks, to stairways and tunnels you must negotiate to reach the platform overhead where trains arrive and depart. Vending machines flank the entrance. On one wall a locked rest room, a ticket booth behind metal screening and dirty glass. Along the opposite wall a bank of rental lockers with and without doors, two benches bolted into the floor that might seat a total of six, if the six were small and very fond of one another. A narrow counter in front of the booth, a few posters and notices on the wall, and that was about it. Unsubtly as a prison cell this place embodies its opinion of you, shouts its message of unwelcome with every corner cut, each unlovely detail, every stain, crack, drip, hole, missing or mutilated feature.

Though I had strolled in at what seemed to be street level, the waiting room is situated underground. A cave in a hillside. Bad light, bad air, the weight of tracks, trains, earth, sky pressing down. Black earth leaching through the thin skin of ceiling and walls, every sweating seam and gritty crack a hole in the dike.

Caves, tunnels, cellars, tenements, back alleys, and backyards, the deserted, seedy, out-of-order back doors of the city, greeting my father and his father, generations of young black men arriving, from South to North, country to town. Would this always be the common ground where we'd meet? Sons and fathers. Fathers and sons.

Train stations, bus stations, the servants' entrance, where you were supposed to slip in and do your grubby business without disturbing the folks moving about in clean, well-lit rooms of the big house.

Who decided things should be this way? Who decreed, and worse, who went along with the program? Clearly the front-door people benefitted from such an arrangement—back doors, front doors, privileged access limited to a few. Why wouldn't they dream it up, demand it if they could get away with demanding. Why wouldn't they fight to hold on if somehow they contrived to seize a monopoly on the front door. But the others, the ones who outnumbered front-door people many, many times over, why were they a party to arrangements keeping them hat in hand, cooling their heels while they tapped gently at the back door. Generation after generation adrift in bus stations, train stations, hitching the highways, foot-slogging through moats of industrial wasteland belting the city's heart.

.   .   .

OUT THE STATION DOOR, HALF A BLOCK AWAY, I couldn't remember whether anyone had been sitting on the benches. Cars still cruising the center of the street. From doorways, alleys, narrow passages between buildings, silhouettes materialized. Women leaned down to talk into car windows or posed on the sidewalk, stylized, frozen as mannequins, or sauntered up and back the same thirty-foot length of pavement, up and back, high-fashion models on a runway, tethered by invisible leashes, displaying what they wore, what they didn't. A car door opens. A women slithers in or hops out, the door slams behind her. In stilt-heeled shoes, crotch-high minis, short shorts, hot pants, tights, they all seemed long-legged and wobbly, unsure of their footing.

Because I was looking for them, I pick them out, in an unlit window, a vestibule at the top of an apartment building's steps, hunkered in a parked car. Same guys I knew from Pittsburgh, the street corners and bars of the Hill District when the Hill was a hot spot where white men out for a good time met black men supplying the goodies. Black men recognizable by their dress, jewelry, their hairdos sometimes, always by the studied nonchalance of word and gesture masking total absorption in the action. Casually camouflaged in hiding places natural to their surroundings, close enough not to miss what's going on, near enough to pounce, removed enough to disappear instantly. Same proprietary caution and vigilance I'd observed in stiff-legged buck antelope surveying their harems on the high plains of Wyoming.

With forty-five minutes or so on my hands I about-face and walk briskly past the station entrance towards a broad intersection. A neon Mardi Gras sign crackles beyond its far corner.

I know exactly where I'm going. What to expect. Naked women and warmish beer in the Mardi Gras. Men drunk or acting drunk or wishing they were drunk hollering, clapping, whistling, throwing money at bare tits and asses jiggling around them. Naked women dancing whose job is to pretend they are having as much fun as the men ogling, yelling insults at them. The off-duty cop, beefy and no-nonsense, collecting a cover charge. A barmaid who instantly spots emptiness on the bar in front of you, takes your order, delivers it in a plastic cup, a smirk on her face that brushes past you or through you, summing up all your compromising secrets.

Going to the Mardi Gras, watching women strip was like gorging on greasy, cholesterol-rich food or playing basketball past the point of exhaustion. A little thinly disguised self-destruction, descent into the pit, mud-wrestling. Down and dirty, indulging unreasonable appetites, not only to punish yourself, but rubbing your nose in mud because your nose enjoyed rooting around in the briar patch, the pot of smells where the body's rainbow ends.

Would my father get a kick out of the Mardi Gras? When I was a young teenager, hadn't he waited tables with his best buddy Chooky Bolden at a club in Shadyside called the Mardi Gras, a club where black customers not welcome in those days, a club where I picked a fight years later for revenge. Would I be embarrassed to ask my father to join me in this Springfield Mardi Gras? If we went together, would it spoil the little rush I might enjoy going alone? What would he think? Of the idea, of the two of us strolling in to check out women's bodies. The joint probably would be closed by the time his train arrives. Would I take him if the place was open? Would I go with my wife, my daughter, my mother?

The Mardi Gras my secret. I couldn't justify its existence nor rationalize spending time or money there. No big deal. Two or three times a year, maybe, if I happened to be in the Springfield area at night, I might detour, order a beer, pay to have my undomesticable erotic fantasies pumped up to virtual reality by live female bodies a few feet from where I sat.

About a third of the time I enjoyed myself. One time in three, I'd split real quickly when I realized a turn-on definitely wasn't about to happen. On those latter occasions the Mardi Gras an instantly depressing turn-off: the women victims, the men assholes, the whole scene pitiful, degrading, contemptible, and people like me who professed to know better and felt superior because we did, yet lined up as customers anyway, deserved to be beaten with a stick. The Mardi Gras about escape. But on a bad night the Mardi Gras a hooting reminder you could never, ever really escape. Your life tailed you everywhere, like a bad credit rating, telling tales, exposing you to strangers, barmaids, the jerk on the stool next to yours, the nude dancer sprawled on her back with her legs wide open, kicking at the ceiling. They could get to you, chase you back into the street because they possessed lives. Lives on view those bad times in the Mardi Gras, lives as raw and public as yours was to them.

Pleasure a third of the time, and another third painful panic, leaving a third compounded of both the above, mixed with one other major ingredient: ambivalence. An uneasy awareness, a funny kind of unpredictable, uncertain give-and-take between pleasure and pain keeping me glued to my seat staring at the women in a numbed daze, wondering what might happen next.

Racism mixed up in it. At a deeper, more tangled, more disquieting, harder-to-talk-about-even-with-myself level than the man/woman politics. Yet inseparable, finally, from gender politics. How many steps from the stage of the Mardi Gras to the auction block. Up or down. Backward or forward.

The one time I'd seen a black dancer in the Mardi Gras I'd avoided her. Dropped my eyes, looked away as I'd taught myself to look away from the nakedness of women in my family. Why did the dancer's color matter? Why was it easier to pretend a white dancer deserved no privacy, that the sanctity of her life in a world beyond the Mardi Gras didn't count? Why wasn't I ashamed of the white dancers when they exposed themselves to the crowd, why didn't it make me feel angry, implicated, ashamed of myself? Sometimes, a third of my time, more or less, I did feel that way. A white dancer triggered the same negative reaction as the black one. Was that a fair measure of my racism? When I noticed the black dancer, and I did quite quickly, my urge was to rescue her, engage her in a long, soulful talk, convince her never to return. Color separated us from almost all the other customers and color suddenly was all that mattered.

If color caused me to respond "decently" to the black dancer, how much did color affect my willingness to exploit and consume the others. And what did this have to do with my wife's color, my erotic life in general, American men and women and sex and color in general.

I remember an image. It didn't appear the night I bumped into the black dancer, but it should have. More like a dream because the image didn't simply flash on and off, but narrated itself, a scenario unfolding as I watched.

A group of men, white men, bobbed along in a lifeboat stranded in the middle of the ocean. They are caricatures, really. Hog-sleek, middle-aged, sunburned CEO types. The hospital gowns they wore could have been togas or expensive business suits and sometimes were. They crowded each other in the tiny rubber raft, yet the raft had once contained tons of booty from a sinking ship they'd destroyed, pillaged, and deserted. In order to survive in the lifeboat, the men had been forced to jettison their misbegotten hoard. They were arguing now about what should go next. The choice was either tossing out their women and children or giving up the illusion they were still in control. Everything else had been fed to the sharks. Even so, the life raft rode lower and lower in the water and the men knew it was only a matter of time, a very brief time indeed, before they joined their scuttled possessions at the bottom of the sea. It had been difficult to give up a lifetime's accumulation of stolen goodies; it hurt, they suffered. The intoxication of playing God, the drug of power, the only item, besides their families, they couldn't bring themselves to surrender, but something had to go to buy a little more time. They voted and decided the illusion of being in charge worth whatever it cost. Women and children overboard.

Plop. Plop. Plop. Not without regret, but the choice is clear. We'll give you anything you want, everything we've denied you when you were our slaves. Here. Take this Volvo. Or this Mercedes. A house on the hill. A yacht. A European vacation. Stocks. Bonds. No, no. Not the old-fashioned kind. Here. These pieces of paper that let you sit on your behind and accumulate fabulous wealth. Take them. Take everything. Just let us alone while we play boss, king, master of the universe.

Yes. Take the children. Color them whatever color you wish. And my women, too. The last straw of their blond hairs. Take the kids I claimed I was breaking my back for, saving for, building my mansions and corporations for. Plop. Plop. Take her too. From the pedestal, fairy tale, love story where I mounted her. The cage whose bars I let you peep through, lust through. Plop.

Rub-a-dub-dub. Image of sad, drowning white men in an empty tub. Each one wearing his captain's hat.

ONE PERSON'S CARNIVAL, ANOTHER PERSON'S MESS TO clean from the streets next morning. I pay my money and step in the Mardi Gras. Just past the counter where the bully collects a cover charge, on a black platform that elevates it to about waist level sits a giant aquarium. A naked woman's inside, her skimpy costume draped over the back wall. Wrinkled bills like some weird variety of sea vegetation scattered on the bottom of the tank. Kneeling, settled back on her haunches, the woman sways sinuously, off time to rock music thumping the club's dark, sooty walls. Track lights smoking in the ceiling blaze into the tank, turn the dancer's flesh starkly white. She sways in wide arcs, outstretched arms undulating, stroking, her fingers splayed to comb the invisible medium through which she glides. I wouldn't have been surprised to see her levitate from the tank's floor, to see rainbow-tinted bubbles seep from her lips. She smiles at no one in particular, enraptured by the undersea ballet she performs, private as the moon's dark side though the crowd presses its nose against the glass, cheers her every move.

When the music stops, she crawls on hands and knees to harvest the money in her Plexiglas cage. She doesn't hurry, doesn't cover up. Wiggles her fanny as she scoots around. Kisses the glass with the cheeks of her ass, close up and personal to the delight of a guy who'd thrown her a handful of bills. I push up closer when she stands at the front of the tank, her weight on one bare foot, leaning so her head, shoulders, and breasts break the plane of the glass wall. Our eyes meet. A smile appears, this time directed at me. She shifts closer to where my hand rests, dangling two dollar bills over the metal-edged wall. I don't know if she intended to brush her skin against my skin or what part of her body she would have allowed to make contact with mine nor how long she might have sustained this intimacy, because the bill-collector bouncer taps me on the shoulder. Huh-uh. That ain't allowed. Stand back, he says. I do.

OUT OF THE MARDI GRAS AS QUICKLY AS I SPLIT THOSE times the vibes all wrong. Fifteen minutes or so before my father's train's due. Maybe it will arrive early. Still no dread. I'm elated by the prospect of seeing him, happy to be awake on a warm fall night at an hour when I'm usually deep in sleep. Grateful for good luck, the power momentarily in my hands to pick him up and deliver him to Amherst. A good car for the ride over the highway. A room secured for him. My good home and bed and wife asleep in it. My son's wedding to share with my father. Daddy my guest now. He could relax, unwind from the train trip, begin luxuriating in VIP treatment. I liked all that and looked forward to speeding through the night, the two of us together, sharing music, the cool night air, whatever we needed to say to each other, what we hadn't gotten around to saying before, words flying back and forth, through the windows and the hole in the roof. Bad air out. Clean air in.

And that's just about what happened:

Hey, mister. How you doing? Good to see you.

You look familiar. Don't I know you from somewhere? I think maybe you do.

Your train a little early.

Haven't been here more than a couple minutes. Just

long enough to walk over there once and look outdoors for you. Boy oh boy, that's one long ride. Feels like I've been riding a week. Glad to see you come through the door.

I thought I was still early. Ride didn't hurt you. You look good. I was here before and left. Thought I was early now.

I'm tired, man. But happy to finally be here.

Lemme take your bag. Car's just outside.

During the ride we chatted like old friends who hadn't seen each other for a very long while. Little stuff, newsy stuff flowed easily, buoyed the conversation, preparing us for the big stuff we'd get around to sooner or later. If we ever did.

BELIEVE IT OR NOT, THE AFTERNOON OF THE WEDDING my father was left behind again. This time at the Country Inn on a Labor Day weekend when the twelve- or fifteen-minute ride from there to my home might require an hour or more in traffic snarled at the Calvin Coolidge Bridge, the headlight-to-taillight creep down Route 9.

The bride's family and guests, some of whom began their journey in Sierra Leone, others in England and Canada, were early for the wedding ceremony. My relatives who'd started out two days before from Pittsburgh were late. I'm not being fair exactly, since nearly all the wedding guests had arrived a day early to attend a dinner honoring bride and groom on the eve of the wedding. Still, my people the late ones today, my family the home team so to speak, and the house full, the magic hour about to strike, and my mother who was staying in the house, the only person from the Pittsburgh contingent in sight.

Not that I had any right to be surprised. I knew my people well enough not to anticipate anything but a last-second appearance. On the basis of who's driving and who's driving the driver, I could accurately predict the order in which the three carloads would arrive. They'd straggle in rather than come in a bunch. Hard enough to get the folks assigned to each vehicle organized, let alone coordinate a simultaneous departure for all the cars. I knew this. Thought of a band of Plains Indians striking their tepees, barking dogs, snorting ponies, kids darting and squealing, everything piled, loaded, strapped down, dust, din, and confusion, as they commence a trek to new hunting grounds, but also the irresistible energy of a natural force, seasons changing, birds migrating. Understood my family would begin arriving one-half minute before or several minutes after the hour printed on the invitations. They'd be late and looking good as they sauntered down the driveway by twos or threes, babies in arms, a flurry of kids in advance. Cool. Not a care in the world. On their own clock they displayed in their smiles, the rhythm of their footsteps on the asphalt, the swaying metronome of their bodies gliding, responding to an ether, a medium, the time they carried within themselves saturating what surrounds them. Inside a bell jar, a vacuum, where the world couldn't touch them. At least as they made their appearance, looking good, looking fine on this grand occasion, their arrival timed to show why the show couldn't really start till they got there.

And so it was. My impatience, annoyance, the little swells of embarrassment as people kept glancing at watches, wagging their heads. The furtive, whispering conferences: shouldn't we wait just a little longer? . . . not fair to everybody else . . . traffic . . . you know they'll be here . . . shouldn't someone call . . . no word yet . . . etc., etc. My eyes straying to the top of the driveway, stung each time no one's there. The audible dull thud of the appointed moment passing and still no sign of Pittsburgh. My head aching to keep my eyes away from the top of the driveway as I circulate and reassure and pretend nothing untoward's occurring—all that mess swept away in an instant by my sister's radiant, Isis smile, the path behind her opening in the sea, my people crossing over, out of time, on time, just in time.

Hi. Hi. Hi.

Scheduled for 1:00, everybody in place at last at 1:55. Except my father.

Daddy's not here. You got to be kidding. We asked him to let us know if he was coming with us. Never heard a word from him.

My brother's a grown man. Knocked on his door when I got up this morning and no answer. He knew our room number.

We were out of there early. Everybody got dressed and went over to the little shopping center to find something to eat. You know. Walked around there awhile afterwards. Ow-whee. It was trifling. Then we drove

straight here. Good thing we did, too, all the traffic we
had to fight. A little late anyway, wasn't we?

The occupants of each car assumed he must be in
another car. Nobody's fault exactly, but nobody had
taken care of business either. The last door slammed of
the last arrival from the Country Inn. No Edgar and I
couldn't believe it. A bad joke and me certainly not in a
laughing mood. Anybody who drove to fetch him would
catch a double whammy coming and going, from the
traffic. Wedding over before they made it back. Two
people missing out instead of one.

The blond, merry-eyed Justice of the Peace seemed to
be enjoying herself, but she was obligated to perform
another wedding later that afternoon so one hour and
fifty-six minutes late the wedding service began. I'd
reached my father at the Country Inn. Once he'd realized
everybody had departed for the wedding, he'd asked the
manager to call a cab. No cabs available without at least
an hour wait on this holiday weekend. The manager had
suggested the airport limo service. In theory a van had
been dispatched to the Country Inn to pick up my father
and express him to Amherst.

My daughter Jamila and my brother-in-law Baron vid-
eotaped the wedding service so I don't need to try to
picture it here. Suffice to say it was short and sweet.
Better than sweet—beautiful. Probably not so short either—beautiful and thus not one moment longer or
shorter than it needed to be. Dan and Maimuna, handsome groom, resplendent bride, had scripted an original
ceremony, a thoughtful, imaginative blend of African and

American customs, including music, poetry, brief addresses, culminating in an exchange of rings. Formality appropriate to the seriousness of their vows, a relaxed spontaneity befitting the spirit of the adventure they'd undertaken together. Traditional fabrics woven in Sierra Leone had traveled across the ocean with Biddy and Roshan, Maimuna's parents. Dashikis and caps for the men, tunics and wraparound skirts for the women, fashioned from the same material. Bright colors in a bold pattern, the sign of two families united on this day.

We had gathered outside on the back deck. Rented chairs in rows, a garland of wild flowers decorating the railing behind a music stand that would serve as a podium and altar. Woods framed the backyard's far end, a border of trees screened neighboring houses. The kind of day Maimuna and Danny must have had in mind when they imagined an outdoor wedding. Clear, bright, crisp, yet pleasantly warm in the sun. A prescience also in the matching colors of our wedding garments: shouting blue for the sky, black and purple for shadows in the thick foliage around us, iridescent silver threads and white hatching for the sunlight that lifted the skin of ordinariness from whatever it touched. A precise, raw insistence in the quality of light, as if it must convey with absolute fidelity to observers at a vast remove the scene in which we participated. For a few moments on the wooden shelf of deck, suspended above the sloping earth at the back of the house, I could almost grasp what it might mean to see and understand with the simple clarity of a distant vision beholding us.

One of my jobs was to serve as a sort of master of ceremonies, opening the program with a welcome to our home, then invoking, as the script instructed, the blessings of the ancestors on the gathering. Since Danny's three surviving grandparents were our closest link to the ancestral spirits, I called upon them to speak first, explaining that my father had been unavoidably delayed, but was expected at any moment.

Almost on cue the breeze stopped. Into this stillness the grandmothers, Elise Goldman and Bette Wideman, spoke. Spoke for themselves and also for the ones absent whose presence grew more palpable in the women's voices. A black woman and a white woman with skin the same color, they shared their enormous strength and dignity. Two mothers, mothers of mothers, themselves daughters, they took us backward and forward, connected us to what we once were, might become, would never be again. In their breath and blood the mystery of time, time unbound by years, time as tangible as it ever gets, materializing in the forms of two women standing before us that afternoon.

Each spoke only a few minutes. Stillness in the air, the neighborhood, held till they were seated again. No sign of my father. On my feet at the music stand, trying to stare through the walls of the house to the top of the driveway, I ad-libbed longer than I should have, then introduced Biddy and Roshan, the bride's parents. A slight, swirling wind kicked up. Leaves twisting, rustling, quick bursts of light.

Biddy, who is also Alhaji Mohammad Badamassie

Mahdi, transported us across the ocean, to African elders living and anciently alive, described tribal rituals, Islamic custom, a gathering and celebration back home in Freetown, Sierra Leone, that would parallel this one. Roshan wore her daughter's beauty and youth in her black eyes. I'm with you, with you, with you, daughter, her eyes whispered, eyes solemn with the sparkle of goblins in them.

Backlit by sunshine as the other speakers had been, Judy in her nimbus of golden light was a stranger I ached to know. Who was this woman, slim, straight-backed, strong, delicate-boned, dark hair falling to her shoulders, hair streaked by shining silver threads that could have been stolen from her elegant dress, its jazz splash of boldly juxtaposed colors, blue black purple silver and white worked by hands an ocean away. I heard in her words a song to the son leaving home, to her dead father she was missing. A song about distance intervening, but closing miraculously, the circle unbroken. It filled her, buoyed her, rising above mellow undertows of pain. I remembered her arms, eyes, nose, cheeks, what was hidden beneath her dress. Recognized her thousand faces in the different one I had discovered that day.

After I spoke, as father not M.C. this time, both Danny's missing grandfathers on my mind. Morty, Judy's father, almost visible beside his wife while she spoke. I'd anticipated his presence and he'd joined us sure enough on this day, reminding Judy of those perfect Maine days he'd loved. Edgar, my father, left behind again, pissed off, anxious, somewhere between the Country Inn and Amherst, missing his chance to speak, to stand before the gathering as an honored elder. Missing the ceremony he'd traveled sixteen hours on the train to witness.

As many varieties of absence as ways of being present, and held up in traffic is not death, but the compartments of the heart are not file drawers, a heart not the place to keep things orderly, neatly stacked and separated. My father stuck somewhere losing this moment was lost to me. I mourned him. A sudden grief so strong it would have shut out the wonder of my son's wedding if I hadn't been able to call upon my father, retrieve the part of him inside myself that could bow, scatter a handful of dust, turn and walk away from the yawning grave.

ABOUT TWENTY MINUTES AFTER THE SERVICE ENDED A king-size van disembarked a passenger at the crest of the driveway of my house on Teaberry Lane. A handsome man, dapper in dark suit, tie, white shirt, and stingy-brim hat, two dashes of moustache on his upper lip, gray fringing his sideburns, a slightly anxious, annoyed expression on his face, hustled out of the vehicle, descended towards the house. He was smiling by the time I met him at the edge of the flagstone walk. I shook his hand, hugged him, saying sorry, sorry, we missed you, as I opened the front door, followed him inside the packed house.

I think he had a ball for the rest of the afternoon and on into the evening, just like the rest of us, eating and drinking too much, dancing, playing instruments, performing skits, teasing, flirting, wisecracking, and gushing, full of ourselves while gifts were unwrapped, cake cut, bride and groom ushered in a shower of rice from the house into their brand-new, beribboned Jeep Scout that would whisk them off for a honeymoon in Maine. A good time had by all, doing the stuff you do at weddings. If my father had been upset at being left behind yet another time, he didn't show it. I figured he was, but he chose to make it nobody's business. The business of the wedding came first, swallowed us all. He was happy, charming. If you weren't aware of what had happened earlier in the day, from his manner, his ease and grin and gracious pride, you would have never guessed he had a perfect right to be sour, brood, curse somebody out. You'd never know.

ALMOST FUNNY IF YOU THOUGHT OF IT IN A CERTAIN way. The extra-long Valley Transporter van, the single passenger. The look crossing my father's face as his feet hit the ground. Dammit. This better be the right goddamn place. At least that's what I might have said in his shined shoes as they hit the asphalt, ignoring the courtesy step the driver had rushed around to place below the sliding door. And I could laugh, did laugh. He'd made it. He was here. I'd learned a few minutes before why parents cry at weddings, so I could laugh now, seeing him hit the ground, hit his determined, nonchalant stride.

The next day, a day my mother reminded me was his birthday, I picked him up at the Country Inn, brought him back to the house. He watched the tape of the wedding Jamila had filmed. I sat with him for part of it and others joined us, coming and going, reliving bits, commenting, signifying. He watched it all, beginning to end. Before he nodded off in the easy chair, I think he might have gotten the hang of the remote-control device and watched some of it again.

Father Stories

One day neither in the past nor future and not this moment either, all the people gathered on a high ridge that overlooked the rolling plain of earth, its forests, deserts, rivers unscrolling below them like a painting on papyrus. Then the people began speaking one by one, telling the story of a life, everything seen, heard, and felt by each soul. As the voices dreamed, a vast, bluish mist enveloped the land and seas below them. Nothing was visible. It was as if the solid earth had evaporated. Now there was nothing but the voices and the stories and the cloud of mist and the people were afraid to stop the storytelling and afraid not to stop because no one knew where the earth had gone.

Finally, when only a few storytellers remained to take a turn, someone shouted: Stop. Enough, enough of this talk. Enough of us have spoken. We must find the earth again.

Suddenly the mist cleared. Below the people the earth had changed.

It had grown into the shape of the stories they'd told, a shape wondrous and new and real as the words they'd spoken. But a world also unfinished because all the stories had not been told.

Some say death and evil entered the world because some of the people had no chance to speak. Some say the world would be worse than it is if all the stories had been told. Some say there are no more stories to tell. Some believe untold stories are the only ones of value and we are lost when they are lost. Some are certain the storytelling never stops and this is one more story and the earth always lies under its blanket of mist being born.

I BEGIN AGAIN BECAUSE I DON'T WANT IT TO END. ALL these father stories that take us back, that bring us here, where you are, where I am, needing to make sense, to go on if we can and should. Your mother said the story she wishes she could write, but knows is so painful she hesitates telling it to herself, would be about her, of course, and you, yes, but also about her father, your grandfather, what he built, who he was, his long, special life, how many other lives he touched, the place he created out of nothing, in the woods, along the lake I'm watching this morning, that watches me as I write.

It was her father she's returned to all these summers in Maine. What he had provided, no strings attached. His gift of water, trees, weather, a world apart full of surprise, a world unchanging. Summers in Maine the stable, rooted part of her.

She told me she'd always run down the steep dirt road, from camp sign to cottage, after the long, hot drive from the city each June when school ended. As soon as her feet hit the Maine ground she knew who she was. Where she wanted to be. The rest of the family might be content to drive down to the cottage. She couldn't wait another second to feel the familiar earth under her. I can see her scooting out of the back seat, grinning. Hear the door slam behind her. She knows exactly where she is. The school year for better or worse a form of exile, time away from where she was supposed to be. In her father's world. Bolting out of the station wagon, the door slamming behind her, braids flying. The woman she must become alive in the quiver and tingle of her bare limbs. The grown-woman parts of her, forgotten as she prances off to be swept up in her father's arms.

I wasn't there. I'm making up the scene but not the connection. This place beside Long Lake a visceral link between father and daughter. As thick as time, as textured and sensuous. A growing into and growing out of, many birthings but each separation enfolded in something larger, richer than a particular moment or mood, something unbreakable.

She was the literal lifeline between her son and her father. She had carried you in her body, the body made from his, so the life she gave to you was also a way of extending the arc of his, and also giving something back to him, the present of you, of your brother and sister, alive, strong, enjoying what he had built, its future, a verification of its past, her father embodied in you, as she's felt since she was a child, her father's presence in all those things—trees, birdsong, shadows, the play of the colors gray and green, the moods of Long Lake that animate this place in Maine she's returned to every summer of her life.

She knew she could always return to Maine because she never really went away. Inside her, safe, sure, was a child running down a green, wooded hill. She could count on that path and count on her father there, wherever else he might be at the moment.

Then everything seemed changed forever. A nightmare haunted her. Another child, a boy, running. Her father's green place shrouded by darkness, frightened child fleeing up an endless black treadmill of hill. Fire the color of blood crackles behind him and he's screaming for help, for her, but there's nothing she can do. Trees, water burning. Her son's hand aflame, igniting the blaze that rages out of control in his wake.

The very ground she loved became undeniable evidence of loss and pain. Burning coals beneath her feet. Countless lines of force converged there, each one a truth, each one splintered, twisted, knotted like the black roots of a giant pine tree upended by lightning.

ONCE, WHEN YOU WERE FIVE OR SIX, ALL THE KEYS TO the camp vehicles disappeared. Keys for trucks, vans, rental cars, a school bus, tractor, boats, the whole fleet necessary each summer to service the business of offering four hundred boys an eight-week escape in the Maine woods. In the innocence of the oasis your grandfather had created, nobody bothered to lock things, keys routinely were left in the ignition for the next driver. Then one day the keys were gone. For hours everybody searched high and low. I thought of you as I climbed into the cab of the dump truck to check for a key that might have fallen to the floor or slipped into some crevice or corner of the raw, gasoline-reeking interior. You because countless times I'd hoisted you into the cab, tucked you in the driver's seat. Nothing you enjoyed more than turning a steering wheel, roaring and vrooming engine noise while you whipped the wheel back and forth, negotiating some endless, dramatic highway only you could see. You were fascinated by that imaginary road and the wheels that rolled you there. Even before you could talk, you'd flip your toy trucks and cars on their sides or upside down so you could spin the wheels, growl motor noise.

You never admitted taking the keys and nobody pressed you very hard after they were found in a heap in the sand under the boat dock, but years later, Junie, the head caretaker, mentioned that he'd seen you making your usual early-morning rounds from vehicle to vehicle the day the keys were missing and confided to me a suspicion he'd felt then, but had kept to himself till you were gone and unlikely to return for a long time. Turns out your grandfather had been suspicious, too. He didn't miss much that happened in the camp either and had observed what Junie had observed. I recall being rather annoyed when your grandfather suggested I ask you if you might have noticed keys anywhere the day they disappeared. Amazed and annoyed because you were hardly more than a baby. No reason for you to bother the keys. I'd instructed you never to touch them, that was one of the conditions you'd promised to honor in return for the privilege of installing yourself behind steering wheels. I trusted you. Questioning my trust insulted us both. Besides, the missing keys implied systematic action, a plot, a prank, sabotage, some scheme premeditated and methodically perpetrated by older campers or adults, and you were just a kid. You were my son. His grandson, so he gently hinted I might casually check with you, not because you were a suspect, but since you had access and had been noticed at the scene, perhaps you might be able to assist the searchers with a clue.

I don't remember your grandfather ever mentioning the keys again until we'd lost you and all of us were searching once more for answers. And since each of us had begun to understand that answers were not around us, not in the air, nor exclusively in you, but inside us all, when your grandfather repeated ten years later his suspicions about the keys, it sounded almost like a confession, and we both understood some searches never end.

A small army of adults, stymied, frustrated, turning the camp inside out. A couple of hours of mass confusion, pockets, drawers, memories rifled, conspiracy theories floated, paranoia blossoming, numb searches and re-searches. Minor panic when duplicate keys weren't stashed where they should be, righteous indignation and scapegoating, the buzz, the edge for weeks afterward whenever keys were mentioned, picked up, or set down in the camp office. The morning of the lost keys became one of those incidents, significant or not in themselves, that lend a name, a tone to a whole camp season: the summer of baby goats in the nature lodge, the hurricane summer, Joey lost for a night on Mount Katahdin, the summer Randy Schwartz bit your grandfather's finger, the summer two counselors from a neighboring boys' camp were killed in a high-speed crash late at night, the Israeli nurses who swam topless, the summer you left and never returned.

If you'd have ambled up on your short, chunky legs and handed me the lost keys, it wouldn't have convinced me you'd taken them. Nor would a confession convince me. Nothing you might have said or done could have solved the mystery of the keys. No accident nor coincidence would have implicated you. Without a reason, with no motive, no *why*, the idea of you removing the keys remained unthinkable.

You were blond then. Huge brown eyes, hair on your head of many kinds, a storm, a multiculture of textures. Kinky, dead straight, curly, frizzy, ringlets, hair thick in places, sparse in others. All your people on both sides of the family ecumenically represented in the golden crown atop your head.

You cried huge tears, too. Heartbreaking, slow, sliding tears that formed gradually in the corners of your dark eyes, gleaming, shapely tears before they collapsed and inched down your cheeks. Big tears, but you cried quietly, almost privately, even though the proof of your unhappiness smearing your face. Then again, when you needed to, you could bellow and hoot. Honking Coltrane explorations of anger, temper, outrage. Most of the time, however, you cried softly, your sobs pinched off by deep, heaving sighs, with a rare, high-pitched, keening wail escaping in spite of whatever it was disciplining you to wrap your sorrow close to yourself.

I'M REMEMBERING THINGS IN NO ORDER, WITH NO PLAN. These father stories. Because that's all they are.

ONE MORNING AS I SIT ON THE DOCK STARING AT THE lake, a man and boy float past in a small boat. They've turned off the putt-putt outboard motor hanging over the stern and are drifting in closer to the rocky shoreline, casting their fishing lines into the water where it's black-ish green from shadows of tall pines lining the lake. A wake spreads languidly behind the boat, one wing plow-ing the dark water, its twin unfurling like a bright flag dragged across the surface. No sound except birdsong, the hiss of a fishing line arching away from the boat, then plopping like a coin in the bottom of a well. The weather has changed overnight. Wind from the west this morn-ing, a cooling, drying wind lifting the mist before dawn, turning the sky unwaveringly blue at this early hour. A wind shunting away last week's mugginess and humidity though it barely ruffles the skin of water in this inlet. Gray bands of different shades and textures stripe the lake's center, panels of a fan lazily unfolding, closing, opening. Later the west wind will perk up and bring chill gusts, stir a chop into the water. Smooth and quiet now for the man and boy hunkered down in their boat. They wear baseball caps, layers of shirts and jackets, the same bulky shape twice, one form larger than the other, each a slightly different color, but identical, down to the way the wrists snap, their lines arc up and away from the boat, the man's lure landing further away than the boy's each time, to scale with the hunched figures drifting past in the boat.

I will see the boat again, about an hour later when the water is louder, when ripples driven from the west are forming scalloped waves. The boy, alone then, whips the boat full throttle in tight, spray-sluicing circles, around and around, gouging deep furrows. The nose of the boat high in the air, he hunches over the screaming engine, gunning it in short, sprinting bursts, then sharp turns, round and round, as if he's trying to escape a swarm of hornets.

The wind is forgetting it's July. I wish for extra insulation under my hooded sweatshirt and nylon windbreaker. Trees are a baffle for the wind and conjure its sound colder, stronger, arctic messages shuttling through the upper atmosphere. Your mother's hair when it's long and loose, catching all the colors of light, falling down around her bare shoulders, carries within itself that windrush of surf crashing far away, the muffled roar of a crowd in a vast, distant stadium.

You'd twist thick clumps of her chestnut hair in your

fist, clutch it while she held you and you sucked the thumb of your other hand. For hours. For hours if she'd let you.

SOMETIMES I FEEL DURATION IS AN ILLUSION—THE SENSE I feel of fifty-two years passing in a blink of an eye a more accurate, plausible reading of simultaneity or whatever time actually might be. Everything happens only once, then everything changes. The notion of duration, of continuity, the possibility of making sense, no more or less than a fragile survival strategy. A hedge against chaos. Nice work if we can get it. The idea that time unfolds linearly in seconds, minutes, hours, years, the terms we've constructed to tame it, feels utterly unconvincing.

Maybe all things happen, including ourselves, long before we see, hear, know they are happening. Consciousness always an afterthought, an attempt to catch up. Our connections to the world a bridge we must cross always slower than the speed of light and the speed of light's truest measure, the present tense. Déjà vu strikes us so powerfully with its uncanny repetitions, its heightened, surreal quality because, ironically, déjà vu is a momentary dead reckoning of what's in fact occurring, an accurate revelation of the tardy alignment of our senses with the world. Déjà vu lifts the veil, tells it like it is. Consider Sartre's metaphor for existence—the passenger fated during the train ride of life to sit facing in the opposite direction of the train's forward motion. Consider the

Akan word *sankofa* for flight with the head turned rearward (to go back and retrieve). Memory then isn't so much archival as it is a seeking of vitality/harmony, an evocation of a truer, more complete, saturated present tense. All this of course relates to personality—the construction of a continuous narrative of self. Our stories. Father stories.

Perhaps one basic source of human unhappiness, perhaps the ingredient some of us sense is missing, even in the good times, follows from this lack of fine-tuning, the inevitable, slightly off lack of correspondence between flow of consciousness and flow of life. *It* goes 45 rpms, we go 33⅓. We record it, not simultaneously but later, never exactly in synch. Out of date, from a distance. Thus, what we get is different music, from a different place and time. Never exactly the original. Alienation, dissatisfaction proceed from the built-in obsolescence of our sense data, our processing machinery. It would/might be great fun to *be* there, but on a microscale, the time it takes to register and process events means we lose a lot of what's happening. Gaps occur. To receive one message requires that we sacrifice others. Time needed for construction destroys the flow, nukes into oblivion everything around it. Measurement influences the system measured, yes, that, but also it disappears what isn't being measured. You work at registering and remembering the first few poorly heard digits of a telephone number someone's reciting over the phone, and in the process miss other digits. Wind up with a jumble of numbers from a message erasing itself while you listen.

Fatheralong

．　　．　　．

DO YOU REMEMBER YOUR FEAR OF LEAVES? OF COURSE
you do. The teasers in our family would never let you
forget.

Once in Laramie, Wyoming, after dinner, just as a
full-moon night was falling and the wide, straight-arrow
streets were empty and still as Long Lake at dawn, I was
riding you on my shoulders, a rare moment, the two of
us together, away from your mother and brother, when
suddenly you cried out. The street we were on had a
ceiling. Branches from trees planted in people's yards
hung over fences lining the sidewalk, forming a canopy
overhead. I panicked. Thought I'd knocked you against a
low branch or you'd gotten your hair tangled, or worse,
been scratched in the eye or face. Your fingers dug into
my scalp. You didn't want to let go as I tried to unseat
you from my shoulders, slide you down into the light
from a street lamp to see what was the matter.

You'd given me a couple good yanks so I was both
mad and scared when I finally pulled you down, cradling
you in my arms to get a clear look at your face.

No tears. No visible damage. Yet you were wild-eyed,
trembling uncontrollably. The leaves had been after you.
Probably not touching you, but worse, a blanket of quiv-
ering, rustling, mottled dread, suddenly hovering above
you. Surrounding you, rendering you speechless. Terror-
ized beyond words or tears, you'd gripped my hair and
kicked my chest. I'd thought you were roughing me up
because you wanted to play. Grabbed your wrists and

squeezed them tight to hold you as I galloped down the quiet Laramie street, doing my best imitation of the bucking bronco on Wyoming license plates. You were rendered even more helpless with your hands clamped in mine, struggling to free yourself while I thought we were having fun. Your father snorting and braying, jiggedy-jig, jiggedy-jig, suddenly in league with your worst enemy, and nowhere to run, nowhere to hide, he was rushing you to your doom. No wonder your fingers tried to rip my hair out when I released your wrists. Holding on, reining me in, pounding on my skull, fighting back the only way you knew how, short of pitching yourself down from a dizzying height, down, down to the pavement, itself strewn with shadowy leaves.

When I was a kid I harbored a morbid fear of feathers. Feathers. Not a single feather or a few loose feathers, like the ones I'd stick in my naps to play Indian, but feathers in a bunch, attached to birds who could wriggle them, flutter them, transform them into loose flesh, rotting, moulting, the unnatural sign of death-in-life and life-in-death, the zombie, mummy, ghost-of-Frankenstein decaying corpses of movies and my nightmares. Feathers a kind of squirmy skin hanging off the bone, all the more horrible because feathers seemed both dry and sticky with blood.

My feathers, your leaves. One afternoon at the Bellmar show on Homewood Avenue, in one of those Bible-days epics, a man was tortured nearly to death, his bloody body flung off a fortress wall. He landed on a heap of corpses in a ditch. As the camera pans the mangled bodies, the sound of huge wings beating thumps through the Bellmar's crackly speakers. After the technicolor glare of carnage under a desert sun, the camera is blinded an instant by the black swoop of vultures. They land atop the corpses, feathers rippling, glinting as the birds commence their slow-motion, ponderously delicate lope towards the choicest morsels of meat—eyeballs, tongues, exposed guts—towards the not-quite-dead-yet man sprawled on a bed of other victims.

Then a closeup of the man's face. As he spots the vultures and screams, I scream. I know I did. Even though I couldn't hear myself because everybody in the Bellmar joined in one shrieking whoop of fear and disgust. And I never forgot the scene. Never. Never forgot, never forgave. Hated pigeons. They became my scapegoat or scapebird. I'd hurt them any chance I got. Trapped one in a box and tormented it. Fully intended to incinerate the crippled one who wound up on the stone steps in the hallway of my dorm freshman year until my roommate shamed me out of it when I asked to borrow his lighter and some fluid and he demanded to know for what.

Pigeons were brown and dirty. They shat everywhere. Spoiled things. Their cooing from the eaves of our roof on Finance Street could startle you awake. They sneaked around, hid in dark corners, carried disease like rats. Far too many of the useless creatures. I focused my fear and hate of feathers on them. Went out of my way to cause them difficulties.

Once I was so angry at your mother's pain, I thought I

was angry at her. She was sharing out loud for the first time how torn apart she'd felt that summer you never came back. How she feared her father's gift had been blighted forever. Woods, lake, sky a mirror reflecting the absence of father, absence of son, the presence of her grief.

I couldn't deal with the pain in her voice so I made up another story. Presumed to tell her she was letting her pain exclude other ways of trying to make sense, with words, with stories, with the facts as given and facts as felt, make sense of the enormity of what happens and doesn't happen, the glimmers of it we paste together trying to find peace. One different story would be the day she meets her father again in this place and what he might have to say to her and why he needed to see her and what he might remind her of and why it would need to be here, on a path through the thick pine woods where light can surprise you penetrating in smoky shafts where it has no business being, where it sparkles then shifts instantly, gone faster than the noises of creatures in the underbrush you never see. I make up her father, as I'm making up mine. Her father appearing to her in a suit of lights because that too could transpire, could redeem, could set us straight in a world where you never know what's going to happen next and often what happens is bad, is crushing, but it's never the worst thing, never the best, it's only the last thing and not even exactly that, except once, and even then death not exactly the last thing that happens because you never know what's going to happen next. For better or worse, cursed and blessed by this ignorance so we invent, fill it, are born with the gift, the need, the weight of filling it with our imaginings. That somehow are as real as we are. Our mothers and fathers and children. Our stories.

I HOPE THIS IS NOT A HARD DAY FOR YOU. I HOPE YOU can muster peace within yourself and deal with the memories, the horrors of the past seven years. It must strike you as strange, as strange as it strikes me, that seven years have passed already. I remember a few days after hearing you were missing and a boy found dead in the room the two of you had been sharing, I remember walking down towards the lake to be alone because I felt myself coming apart, the mask I'd been wearing, as much for myself as for the benefit of other people, was beginning to splinter. I could hear ice cracking, great rents and seams breaking my face into pieces, carrying away chunks of numb flesh. I found myself on my knees, praying to a tree. In the middle of some absurdly compelling ritual I'd forgotten I carried the memory of. Yet there I was on my knees, digging my fingers into the loose soil, grabbing up handfuls, sinking my face into the clawed earth as if it might heal. Speaking to the roots of a pine tree as if its shaft might carry my message up to the sky, send it on its way to wherever I thought my anguish should be addressed.

I was praying to join you. Offering myself in exchange for you. Take me. Take me. Free my son from the terrible things happening to him. Take me in his place. Let them happen to me. I was afraid you were dying or already dead or suffering unspeakable tortures at the hands of a demon kidnapper. The tears I'd held back were flowing finally, a flood that brought none of the relief I must have believed hoarding them would earn me when I let go at last. Just wetness burning, clouding my eyes. I couldn't will the spirit out of my body into the high branches of that tree. What felt familiar, felt like prayers beside my bed as a child, or church people moaning in the amen corner, or my mother weeping and whispering *hold on, hold on* to herself as she rocks side to side and mourns, or some naked priest chanting and climbing towards the light on a bloody ladder inside his chest, these memories of what might have been visions of holiness could not change the simple facts. I was a man who most likely had lost his son, and hugging trees and burying his face in dirt and crying for help till breath slunk out of his body wouldn't change a thing.

A desperate, private moment, one of thousands I could force myself to dredge up if I believed it might serve some purpose. I share that one example with you to say the seven years have not passed quickly. The years are countless moments, many as intense as this one I'm describing to you, moments I conceal from myself as I've hidden them from other people. Other moments, also countless, when terrible things had to be shared, spoken aloud, in phone calls with lawyers, depositions, interviews, conferences, in the endless conversations with your mother. Literally endless because often the other business of our lives would seem merely a digression from the dialogue with you, about you. A love story finally, love of you, your brother and sister, since no word except love makes sense of the ever-present narrative our days unfold.

Time can drag like a long string, studded and barbed, through a fresh wound so it hasn't gone quickly. The moment-to-moment, day-by-day struggles imprint my flesh, but the seven years also a miracle, a blink of the eye through which I watch myself wending my way from there to here. In this vast house of our fathers and mothers.

YOUR MOTHER DIDN'T NEED MY WORDS OR IMAGES TO work out her grief. She needed time. Took the time she needed to slowly, gradually, painstakingly unravel feelings knotted in what seemed for a while a hopeless tangle. No choice really. She's who she is. Can give nothing less than her whole heart to you, to this place inseparable from all our lives her father, your grandfather, provided.

For a while I guess it must have felt impossible. And still can, I know. She may have doubted her strength, her capacity to give enough, give everything because everything seemed to be tearing her apart, breaking her down. She needed time. Not healing time exactly, since certain wounds never heal, but time to change and more time to learn to believe, to understand she could go on, was going on for better or worse. She could be someone she'd never dreamed she could be. Her heart strong, whole, even as it cracks and each bit demands everything.

THE FULLNESS OF TIME. THE FULLNESS OF TIME. THAT phrase has haunted me since I first heard it or read it, though I don't know when or how the words entered my awareness, because they seem always to have been there, like certain melodies, for instance, or visual harmonies of line in your mother's body, I wonder how I've ever lived without, the first time I encountered them, although another recognition clicked in almost simultaneously, reminding me that I'd been waiting for those particular notes, those lines, a very long time. They'd been forming me before I formed my first impressions of them.

The fullness of time. Neither forward nor backward. A space capacious enough to contain your coming into and going out of the world, your consciousness of these events, the wrap of oblivion bedding them. A life, the passage of a life, the truest understanding, measure, experience of time's fullness. So many lives and each different, each unknowable, no matter how similar to yours, your flesh and not your flesh, lives passing, as yours, into the fullness of time, where each of these lives and all of them together make no larger ripple than yours, all and each abiding in the unruffled innocence of the fullness that is time. All the things that mattered so much to you or them sinking into a dreadful, unfeatured equality that is also rest and peace, time gone but more always more, the hands writing, the hands snatching, hands becoming bones then dust then whatever comes next, what time takes and fashions of you after the possibilities, permutations and combinations, the fullness in you is exhausted, played out for the particular shape it's assumed for a time in you, for you, you are never it, but what it could be, then is not, you not lost but ventured, gained, stretched, more, until the dust is particles and the particles play unhindered, unbound, returned to the fullness of time.

I KNOW MY FATHER'S NAME, *EDGAR*, AND SOME OF HIS fathers' names, *Hannibal, Tatum, Jordan*, but I can't go back any further than a certain point, except I also know the name of a place, Greenwood, South Carolina, and an even smaller community, Promised Land, nearly abutting Greenwood, where my grandfather, who's of course your great-grandfather, was born, and many of his brothers are buried there under sturdy tombstones bearing his name, our name, *Wideman* carved in stone in the place where the origins of the family name begin to dissolve into the loam of plantations owned by white men, where my grandfathers' identities dissolve, where they were boys, then men, and the men they were fade into a set of facts, sparse, ambiguous, impersonal, their intimate lives unretrievable, where what is known about a county, a region, a country and its practice of human bondage, its tradition of obscuring, stealing, or distorting black people's lives, begins to crowd out the possibility of seeing my ancestors as human beings. The powers and principalities that originally restricted our access to the life free people naturally enjoy still rise like a shadow, a wall between my grandfathers and myself, my father and me, between the two of us, father and son, son and father.

So we must speak these stories to one another.

                    Love.